Normative Economics

NORMATIVE ECONOMICS

An introduction to microeconomic theory and radical critiques

Frank J. B. Stilwell
University of Sydney

PERGAMON PRESS

Pergamon Press (Australia) Pty Limited, P.O. Box 544, Potts Point, N.S.W. 2011
Pergamon Press Ltd, Headington Hill Hall, Oxford OX3 OBW
Pergamon Press Inc., Fairview Park, Elmsford, NY 10523
Pergamon Press SARL, 24 rue des Ecoles, 75240 Paris
Pergamon Press GmbH, 3300 Braunschweig, Burgplatz 1

First published 1975

© 1975 Frank J. B. Stilwell

Cover design by Allan Hondow

Printed by Dai Nippon Printing Co. (Hong Kong) Ltd.

Stilwell, Frank J. B.
    Normative economics: an introduction to microeconomic theory and radical
    critiques/ [by] Frank J. B. Stilwell—Rushcutters Bay, N.S.W.:
    Pergamon Press, 1975.
    Index.
    ISBN 0 08 018300 x.

    1. Economics. I. Title.

    330

To my parents

Contents

	Preface	*ix*
I	Perspectives	*1*
II	To Whom?	*12*
III	How?	*35*
IV	What?	*53*
V	Where?	*75*
VI	When?	*90*
VII	Public Policy	*104*
VIII	Radical Alternatives	*119*
	Author Index	*141*
	Subject Index	*145*

Preface

The orthodox approach to economics has recently come under attack from many different directions. Some economists have pointed to problems arising from internal inconsistencies in the analysis. More generally, the criticism has been of the irrelevance of the orthodox approach to the solution of modern economic problems. Students increasingly have voiced their concern over the failure of the theory to help them understand the economy in which they live. The emphasis on entrepreneurial behaviour, competition and equilibrium, is seen as being of little relevance in an economy dominated by giant corporations, collusive behaviour and tendencies to cumulative disequilibrium. But dissent is not limited to undergraduates. Some of the world's most eminent economists have voiced deep concern over the current irrelevance of orthodox economics.

However, this criticism has not yet been incorporated into the standard textbooks. This book seeks to help overcome the problem by introducing students to economics in a critical way. The intention is that the reader should be made familiar with orthodox techniques, but at the same time he or she should be shown the limitations and ideological underpinnings of those techniques. The approach differs from that of other books in economics mainly in that it is critical and explicitly normative. The normative dimension is particularly important to emphasise. The trend in economics in the last couple of decades has been to play down the role of value-judgements in an attempt to construct a positive economics, free of any personal or social-class bias. The objective is worthy enough, but it has proved to be unattainable. As we shall see throughout the book, value-judgements enter economics in a variety of ways and they do so in a systematic and generally class-biased manner. They enter in the selection of assumptions on which theories are based, and even in the selection of economic problems to investigate. The result is that much of orthodox economics serves an apologetic rather than a purely scientific function.

The emphasis of this book is largely on microeconomics, though some elements of macroeconomics intrude from time to time. The book is designed principally for university students taking courses in microeconomics, welfare economics and general economic principles. However, it may also be suitable for use by secondary-level students, since the exposition is non-technical and assumed knowledge is negligible.

The book begins with a general discussion of economic problems, the approach taken by orthodox economics and the standards by which economic analysis may be judged.

The next three chapters deal with the more conventional dimensions of microeconomic analysis, but the orthodox theories are given a very critical scrutiny, particularly with respect to the reasonableness of their underlying assumptions. Also, attention is paid to equity as well as efficiency considerations. These chapters seek to develop an overall appraisal of the extent to which the market economy generates the ideal outcome in relation to what is produced, how it is produced and to whom it is distributed.

The following two chapters deal with dimensions of economic allocation problems which are equally important but usually omitted from books on microeconomics. These are the consideration of where economic activities are located and when they occur. Introducing these dimensions gives an opportunity for discussing current issues such as congestion in cities, pollution and the social costs of economic growth.

The book ends with two chapters on remedial measures. The first considers the orthodox liberal position and examines the arguments for government policies to control monopoly, redistribute income and so on. The second outlines the radical approach which sees the government as an instrument of class-domination and hence, as part of the economic problem.

This general structure is quite conservative in the sense that the bounds of the subject are taken as those set down by orthodox economics. Part of the radical critique of this orthodoxy is that these bounds are too narrowly set. For example, a common charge made by radicals is that more emphasis needs to be placed on problems of 'resource creation' as opposed to problems of resource allocation. Also, orthodox economics is often criticised because of its neglect of social and cultural considerations in the analysis and appraisal of economic systems. This book is not centrally concerned with such matters, important though they undoubtedly are in an overall appraisal of the state of economics. Rather, the emphasis is on the value of orthodox economic analysis in dealing with the particular questions for which it has been developed. This is what is meant by describing the framework as conservative. However, within this framework the approach taken is generally of a radical nature.

This is particularly true of the final chapter which may be read independently of the rest of the book as an indication of the different emphasis of radical economics.

I am grateful to Evan Jones for very useful comments on an earlier draft of the book, and to Mary Deane who did the typing.

FRANK J. B. STILWELL

Sydney, September 1974.

CHAPTER ONE

Perspectives

Economics and Social Objectives

What are economic systems for? An economic system like any other system, is a means of organisation for achieving particular ends. So, some statement about social objectives is clearly necessary if we are to develop a framework for analysing and appraising economic systems. Indeed, without such a statement it is impossible to identify economic problems, since problems imply failure to achieve particular goals. However, consensus on goals is not easy to find. The answer to the question 'What are economic systems for?' depends wholly on whom you ask. The existence of poverty, for example, is clearly and painfully recognised as a problem by some, while others do not see the removal of poverty as a major function of the economic system. Similarly, some groups within the community are intensely concerned with the problem of environmental degradation, while others are unconcerned, either because they are relatively unaffected by the degradation or because they actually profit from it.

In these circumstances, an economist who is concerned with the assessment of economic systems and with helping to solve economic problems has a choice between limited alternatives: he or she may accept the role of 'hired hand', accept the 'values of the ballot-box', or attempt to devise a set of 'independent' standards of evaluation.

Let us look a little more closely at these options. The first requires that the economist subordinates his or her value-judgements to the person or institution for whom he or she works. He or she becomes a purely technical advisor. The employer may be a political party, a business corporation, a citizens' action group or whatever. The economist in these circumstances, in effect, adopts the value-judgements of his employer. This is very neat, but not very satisfactory. The economist has not avoided making a value-judgement; it is embodied in the decision about whom to work for! If he or she simply works for the highest bidder, then a value-judgement has been made that the price system allocates resources to their proper uses. On the other hand, if an economist offers his or her services to a citizens' action group rather than a business corporation, that normally embodies a different value judgement, that those with least power are the most deserving of help.

Somewhat similar problems are associated with the second alternative, of accepting the 'values of the ballot-box'. The approach requires the economist to accept the value judgements revealed by the existing political institutions. Of course, one's confidence in this approach depends largely on one's confidence in the political institutions; and the imperfections of political institutions as a means of revealing what is best for the community are widely recognised. In some cases there is no 'ballot-box', so one must face the choice of whether or not to serve the particular totalitarian régime in power. In other cases, the representative nature of the government may be in doubt, either because of 'gerrymandering' in relation to electoral boundaries or because of Watergate-type incidents which reveal the dishonesty of the elected representatives. Suffice it to say that political scientists have severe reservations about the ability of political institutions to reveal any sort of 'general will', and that in these circumstances an economist does not eschew value-judgements by serving those institutions. The approach has a built-in bias towards the *status quo*: if one takes the values thrown up by the existing political system, whether it be democratic or totalitarian, one necessarily serves (and helps to legitimise) the existing social order.

The third alternative, of independently listing standards of evaluation, is the most honest approach an economist can make and the one least subject to the problem of bias towards the *status quo*. In effect, the economist makes a personal statement of value-judgements and uses that as a basis for the analysis and evaluation of economic systems. If nothing else, this approach enables one to readily identify the extent to which differences between economists are due to differences in fundamental value-judgements as distinct from other sources of disagreement.

The main problem facing an economist in preparing such a statement is that of deciding how broadly based such a listing should be. Should it be limited to fairly specific and readily quantifiable matters or should it include social objectives which are not amenable to quantitative evaluation? This problem is the more acute because of possible conflicts between such standards. For example, to achieve the highest attainable level of material well-being may require a form of social and economic organisation in which cultural activity cannot flourish. If this is so, then the more narrowly defined the set of objectives the greater the likelihood of problems arising because conflicts such as this are ignored. The best approach would seem to be to specify a very broad set of criteria for analysing systems and subsequently try to specify trade-offs between the various norms. This is the approach which has been taken up most enthusiastically by the so-called radical political economists. Herb Gintis, for example, has suggested the following set of criteria by which economic systems may be appraised.

(1)   material well-being;
(2)   equity;
(3)   responsiveness of institutions to human needs and historical characteristics of a society;
(4)   human development.[1]

This list may be extended by the addition of other criteria. The following two have also been suggested:

(5)   community development;
(6)   harmony of man in his natural environment.

The former could be considered to be encompassed by Gintis' fourth category but is usefully separated because of the emphasis on community values which interact with, but are not necessarily always compatible with, the interests of individual members of the community. Similarly, the latter is not fully covered by Gintis' third category because of the different emphasis on accommodating to the environment rather than modifying the environment through institutional changes. Clearly the list is by no means definite, but serves to illustrate the broad range of objectives which a social scientist may consider potentially relevant in the assessment of economic systems and their associated institutions.

However, this approach is not typical. It is more normal to find in the writings and speeches of economists and the politicians they advise, an almost exclusive concern with the objective of maximising the aggregate volume of production. The following quotation from an early book by the American economist J. K. Galbraith makes the point forcefully: 'In the Autumn of 1954, during the Congressional elections of that year, the Republicans replied to Democratic attacks on their stewardship by arguing that this was the second best year in history. It was not, in all respects, a happy defence. Many promptly said that second best was not good enough—certainly not for Americans. But no person in either party showed the slightest disposition to challenge the standard by which it is decided that one year is better than another. Nor was it felt that any explanation was required. No one would be so eccentric as to suppose that second best meant second best in the progress of the arts and sciences. No one would assume that it referred to health, education, or the battle against juvenile delinquency. There was no suggestion that a better or

[1]   See the discussion in E. Behr, V. Garlin, J. Morris and R. Roehl, *Towards a Radical Political Economics, The Review of Radical Political Economics*, July, 1971, pp. 17-42.

poorer year was one in which the chances for survival amidst the radioactive furniture of the world had increased or diminished. Despite a marked and somewhat ostensible preoccupation with religious observances at the time, no one was moved to suppose that 1954 was the second best year as measured by the number of people who had found enduring spiritual solace. Second best could mean only one thing—that the production of goods was the second highest in history.'[2]

More recently, the British economist E. J. Mishan has expressed similar scepticism about the narrow definition of economic objectives: 'Even the younger men of today, struggling for the reins of power, habitually disregard, in their diagnoses of the times, the new sources of social conflict and social discontent emerging around us. . . . One factor that enables them to get away with their routine push-and-shove exhortation to the public is the postwar "discovery" of that latest addition to the armoury of the Establishment, the economic index. A remarkably simple thing in itself, a mere number in fact, yet one that is treated with unabashed reverence. Apparently one has but to consult it to comprehend the entire condition of society. Among the faithful, and they are legion, any doubt that, say, a 4 per cent growth rate, as revealed by the index, is better for the nation than a 3 per cent growth rate is near-heresy; it is tantamount to a doubt that four is greater than three.'[3]

There is clearly a fundamental conflict here. Economic systems should be appraised according to their success in serving a very wide range of social objectives, yet in practice the appraisal is often crudely one-dimensional. The reasons for this situation are complex. A full understanding would require an analysis of the ways in which ideas about economic systems are developed and how they are expressed in political institutions and disseminated through the media. The following section explores just one aspect—one that is crucially important to us as students of economics—the role of economic theory.

The Focus of Orthodox Economics

Economic theory in the twentieth century has been dominated by one particular school of thought, variously known as neo-classical economics, mainstream economics and orthodox economics. Indeed, the dominance of this school has been so complete that it has often been simply called 'economics'. However, it is a body of thought which is quite restricted in a number of ways.

Firstly, it has been developed largely as an analysis of one particular economic system, the capitalist system. This is a system with many variants but its two

[2] J. K. Galbraith, *The Affluent Society*, Harmondsworth, Penguin Books, 1962, p. 107.
[3] E. J. Mishan, *The Costs of Economic Growth*, Harmondsworth, Penguin Books, 1969, p. 19.

general features are the private ownership of property and the allocation of resources through a market system. This is just one type of economic system; others include primitive communal, feudal and socialist. The socialist system has been of growing importance in the twentieth century and well over one-third of the world's population now live in countries characterised by socialist forms of economic organisation. Like capitalism, socialism has many variants. Its main features are an emphasis on collective ownership of property and on the allocation of resources through administrative decisions. In some cases the contrast between capitalism and socialism is not striking, in that some capitalist systems feature a quite high degree of government intervention and planning in the economy, while some socialist-based systems make restricted use of market mechanisms. However, an essential difference remains in that economic structure of capitalism is dominated by private capital whereas socialist economies rely on collective decision-making to determine the main structure of economic activity.

Naturally enough, the economic theory developed by capitalist economists for capitalist systems has emphasised the role played by the market in the allocation of resources. Of particular importance is the emphasis on price determination in different types of market situation, because prices are the signals which indicate the most profitable use to which a resource can be put. Indeed, the price system is a remarkably simple device. In ideal circumstances it ensures that resources always flow to their most productive use and that goods always end up in the hand of those who express the strongest demand for them. When the number of potential users of any resource exceeds the amount available, the price associated with that particular resource rises, thus ensuring that it is used by the highest bidder. This price rise will have the secondary effect of acting as a signal to suppliers and potential suppliers of the resource: they will plan to expand supply in the future in order to profit from the new situation. Thus, demand increases cause increases in supply to serve those expanded demands. Conversely, demand reductions bring about supply reductions because of the reduced price prevailing in the market. In this way, prices act as an equilibrating mechanism and remove the possibility of gluts and shortages in particular markets.

It is the simplicity of this allocation process that has given it much of its appeal to economists. The price system is certainly a fantastic 'fine-tuning' mechanism. Resources flow from uses where their price is low to where their price is high in a continual adjustment to changes in the pattern of demand and the technological production possibilities. Bureaucratic control is redundant since such an ideal price system is more sensitive than any administrative body to the stimuli of economic changes. No wonder that so many economists have been awestruck by the aesthetic harmony and elegance of this method of resource allocation!

But there is a danger in all this. Markets in practice are seldom perfect. Monopoly buyers and sellers are not uncommon, and even when complete monopoly is not present, collusion between buyers or sellers can have a similar effect. Information about available alternatives may not be readily obtainable. Rigidities may also occur in the form of resource immobility. Some economists have gone so far as to argue that for the largest sector of modern capitalist economies, that dominated by giant corporations, the market has been partially replaced by planning as the principal means of resource allocation. In these circumstances, to continue to focus economic theory on price formation and resource allocation through the market, may not be particularly helpful. Papandreau puts the point strongly: 'to extend, unwittingly or not, the analytical conclusions of a model best fitted for the study of a shopkeeper society to present-day capitalism is probably the supreme form of ideological bias'.[4]

Orthodox economics has some other features which restrict its scope. We have seen that it is particularly oriented towards capitalist systems and that it places major emphasis on the workings of the market as a means of resource allocation. But (and here we come back to the issue of social objectives again) it is an almost exclusively efficiency-oriented analysis. As such, it is of potential value in analysing how the system serves the objective of securing a high level of material well-being. But it can tell us very little about the other aspects which are relevant in the assessment of economic systems. The neglect of equity considerations poses a particular problem. The whole of orthodox economics takes the existing distribution of wealth as given, as determined outside the system. This is a major limitation because the distribution of wealth in reality is determined by economic phenomena and in turn has an important impact on the way in which economic systems operate. We shall have occasion to return to this point on a number of occasions later in this book.

Let us now look in some more detail at the major internal sub-divisions within orthodox economics.

Textbooks typically begin with the distinction between the economic functions of resource utilisation (maintaining full employment of resources), resource allocation (securing an optimal allocation between alternative uses), and resource growth (achieving a satisfactory rate of material progress).

The distinction between the three can be most easily illustrated in terms of the *production possibility frontier*. The formal derivation of this concept will

[4] A. G. Papandreau, *Paternalistic Capitalism*, Minneapolis, University of Minnesota Press, 1972, p. 40.

be considered later in this book, but its significance is quite easy to grasp, and it is useful to introduce it at this stage. The conventional illustration involves the choice between guns and butter as shown in *Figure 1.1*.

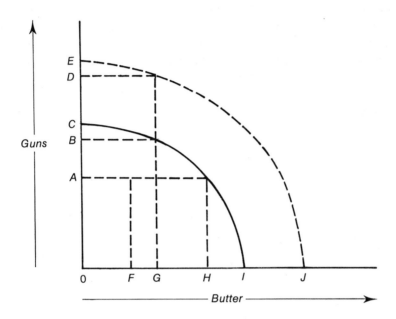

Figure 1.1 The production possibility frontier

If all society's resources were allocated to armourment production, the number of guns that could be produced is represented by *OC*. If they were all used in making butter, the amount of butter that could be produced is represented by *OI*. Probably some intermediate position, where both guns and butter are produced, will normally occur. A line connecting *C* to *I* represents these possibilities and is known as the production possibility frontier. If all resources are equally suited to both gun and butter production then this line would be perfectly straight: the one in *Figure 1.1* is shown as concave to the origin to indicate that not all resources are equally suited to both uses. Any point on this frontier is possible: for example, the society could produce *OB* guns and *OG* butter or *OA* guns and *OH* butter. Which combination to produce is a decision of *resource allocation*.

Now, if society actually produces some combination within the frontier (say *OA* guns and *OF* butter) then resources are not fully used. In order to expand the production of guns it would not be necessary to contract butter production, as it would if you were initially at some point on the frontier.

More of both goods can be produced. In this situation, there is said to be *resource underutilisation.*

A move to some point of the frontier eliminates such waste of resources.[5] However, the society cannot achieve any combination of guns and butter outside the frontier with the existing resources at its disposal. To produce *OD* guns plus *OG* butter would require an expansion of resources (either land, labour, capital, or the efficiency with which those inputs are combined). The process of resource growth shifts the production possibility frontier outward to some new position such as shown in *Figure 1.1* by the dotted line *EJ*. This process of expansion is what is meant by the third aspect of orthodox economics, *resource growth.* This aspect is essentially different from the utilisation and allocation aspects because it is a dynamic process, involving change over time, whereas utilisation and allocation are essentially static, concerned with the use of resources at a given moment in time.

In addition to these three major aspects of economic objectives frequent reference is also made to two other economic objectives, relating to external balance and inflation. However, these two objectives may be considered to be of a secondary nature: not only are they mutually interrelated but they also have close links with the problems of utilisation, allocation and growth. Thus, if a country experiences a very rapid rate of inflation, this is likely to cause balance of payments problems because goods become increasingly difficult to sell abroad due to their high prices, while imports will increase because of their low prices relative to domestically produced goods. These balance of payments difficulties are likely to lead to deflationary policies which cause short-run unemployment and put a brake on long-run growth trends. In this way, attempts to achieve stable prices and external balance objectives may influence the attainment of the other objectives. For this reason it is possible to regard balance of payments and inflation objectives as ancillary to those of resource utilisation, allocation and growth. Their importance stems from their effects on the ease of attaining the three more fundamental objectives.

We have now identified a primary classification of the subject-matter of orthodox economics, resource utilisation, allocation and growth. This is reflected roughly in the major conventional decision within the discipline. Resource utilisation is the prime focus of *macroeconomics.* Particularly since the pathbreaking work in the 1930's of John Maynard Keynes (later to become Lord Keynes), large number of economists have addressed themselves to the question of how capitalist systems can be managed so as to ensure that major

---

[5] Note, however, that we cannot say that a point on the frontier is 'better' than one inside it unless we make a value-judgement about the desirability of more commodities. (Remember, nuclear weapons are a commodity!)

resource underutilisation does not occur. They have also addressed themselves, though with less success, to the related question of how to control inflation while maintaining low rates of resource underutilisation. The allocation issue has been the focus of *microeconomics* and the related discipline called *welfare economics*. Resource growth has been the focus of a third, more fuzzily-bounded area of the subject. Most of the so-called economics of development comes in this last category, as does the historically-oriented analysis of growth undertaken by investigators such as Kuznets and Denison.[6]

This book is largely about resource allocation, and subsequent chapters make only occasional mention of problems of utilisation and growth. What this amounts to saying is that orthodox microeconomics and welfare economics defines the scope of this book, with the clear exception of the last chapter where broader perspectives are introduced.

Nevertheless, narrow as this scope is in relation to the potential subject area of economic analysis, it does involve the study of some very interesting questions. Five groups of resource allocation problems may be identified:

(1) to whom? (analysis of how the pattern of distribution of goods and services is determined);

(2) how? (analysis of how the methods by which goods and services are produced is determined);

(3) what? (analysis of how the composition of the output of goods and services is determined);

(4) where? (analysis of how the location of economic activities is determined);

(5) when? (analysis of how the allocation of economic activities over time is determined).

These are the main dimensions of the resource allocation problem. Orthodox economics has paid most attention to the first three aspects, but there has been growing interest in the last two aspects, particularly as a result of the debate on the social and environmental consequences of rapid economic growth and urbanisation.

Strictly speaking, some of these matters are not purely concerned with resource allocation. Inter-temporal allocation problems often involve considerations of resource growth, while some aspects of resource utilisation are raised, for example, in relation to the effect of alternative spatial allocations in creating localised unemployment. Perhaps most important of all, considerations of equity are of central importance in our discussion of the

---

[6] See S. Kuznets, *Economic Growth of Nations*, Cambridge, Mass., Harvard University Press, 1971 and E. F. Denison, *Why Growth Rates Differ*, Washington D.C., The Brookings Institution, 1967.

'to whom' dimension of resource allocation.

Nevertheless, the general classification provides a useful framework within which to appraise the performance of economic systems in relation to material objectives. The framework is summarised in *Figure 1.2*.

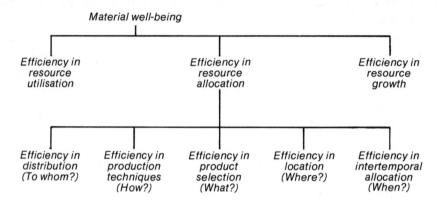

Figure 1.2   A scheme of conventional economic objectives

This defines the structure of this book. The various dimensions of resource allocation and the orthodox economic theory which attempts to explain how these matters are resolved are considered in Chapters 2 to 6. The final two chapters then look at implications for public policy and some broader perspectives.

Appraisal of Economic Analysis

We have identified the area of study. How are we to appraise the adequacy of economic theory in handling the subject area in question?

This is an important methodological question and one which has caused deep and often bitter divisions among economists. Let us start with a point of agreement. All economists agree that some generalisations must be made. As Boulding has noted: 'Knowledge is always gained by the orderly loss of information, that is, by condensing and abstracting and indexing the great buzzing confusion of information that comes from the world around us into a form we can appreciate and comprehend'.[7] Similarly, Duesenbury says, 'Knowing how to simplify one's description of reality without neglecting anything essential is the most important part of an economist's art'.[8]

[7] K. Boulding, *Economics As A Science*, New York, McGraw-Hill, 1970, p. 2.
[8] J. S. Deusenbury, *Business Cycles and Economic Growth*, New York, McGraw-Hill, 1958, pp. 14-15.

Such simplifications require that certain assumptions be made about economic behaviour. Indeed, it is inherent in the process of theorising that the analysis be based on assumptions. However, there are important differences between economists as to the importance of the realism of these assumptions. On the one hand, Friedman argues that: 'A theory cannot be tested by comparing its assumptions directly with reality . . . (rather) a hypothesis can only be tested by the conformity of its implications or predictions with observable phenomena'.[9] On the other hand, Rotwein contends that 'What we seek in science is not merely "prediction" in the Friedman sense of the term—which is the prediction of the crystal ball—but prediction through "explanation". Only this enables us to construct a deductive system involving the real world which can make this world intelligible to us.'[10]

Probably the most balanced attitude is that of Baran and Sweezy: 'When we finally get our model, there is one test to which we must subject it: does it help to make sense of the real world? Or, to put the matter another way, does it help us to see connections to which we were previously blind, to relate effects to causes, to replace the arbitrary and the accidental by the regular and the necessary? In a word, does it help us to understand the world and act in it intelligently and effectively?'[11]

This last view is the one on which the evaluation of economic analysis in this book is based. Overall, it seems reasonable to require of economic models that they be based on assumptions which are not clearly in conflict with generally observable features of the real economic system.

[9] M. Friedman, The Methodology of Positive Economics, in *Essays in Positive Economics*, Chicago, University of Chicago Press, 1953.

[10] E. Rotwein, Some Methodological Questions and the Theory of the Firm (mimeographed), cited in J. W. McGuire, *Theories of Business Behaviour*, Englewood Cliffs NJ, Prentice-Hall Inc., 1964. For a detailed critique of the Friedman position, see E. Nagel, Assumptions in Economic Theory, *The American Economic Review*, May 1963, pp. 211-219.

[11] P. Baran & P. Sweezy, *Monopoly Capital*, Harmondsworth, Penguin Books, 1968, pp. 27-28.

CHAPTER TWO

To Whom?

This chapter is concerned with developing a theory of commodity distribution and exchange. Can one distribution be said to be more efficient than another? Is there any conflict between efficient distribution and equitable distribution? How does the price system compare with other methods of 'slicing up the economic cake' according to these efficiency and equity criteria? Such questions as these are of fundamental importance, not only in the development of economic analysis but in current political debate about whether things such as health, education and transport services should be distributed through a price system or through some other means.

Techniques for Analysing Distributional Efficiency

Let us begin by looking at what orthodox theory says about identifying an efficient distribution of commodities between consumers. Consider the very simplest case: an economy featuring two consumers who (following a well-developed tradition) we call Robinson Crusoe and Man Friday, and two commodities, bread and wine. The amount of bread and wine available is assumed to be fixed (perhaps representing the amount salvaged from Crusoe's ship before it sank). We can represent this situation diagrammatically by what is called an *Edgeworth box* (named after the economist Francis Edgeworth). This is shown in *Figure 2.1*.

The dimensions of this box can be easily related to the production possibility frontier introduced in the previous chapter. The selection of any point on the frontier determines the amount of the two commodities available for distribution. In effect, our assumption of a fixed amount of bread and wine available for distribution, is the same as assuming that the 'what?' decision has already been taken. If the supply of bread and wine is denoted by point R on the production possibility frontier in *Figure 2.2*, then the Edgeworth box is shown by $OBRC$. If the supply of bread and wine is shown by point S, then its dimensions are $OASD$.

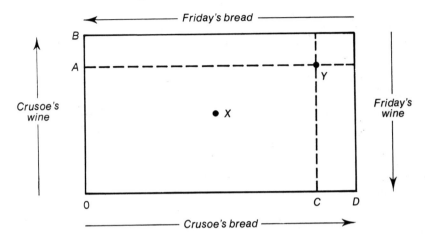

Figure 2.1   The Edgeworth box

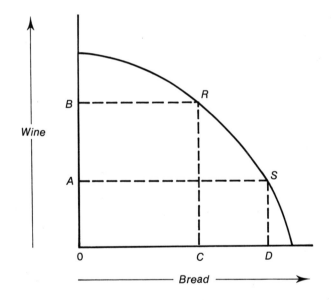

Figure 2.2   The relationship between the production possibility frontier and the Edgeworth box

Now let us look back to *Figure 2.1*. The height of the box (*OB*) represents the amount of wine available to be shared between the two consumers. The quantities going to Crusoe and Friday can be measured in opposite directions on this axis, since what one does not consume is available for the other. Thus, if Crusoe takes *OA*, then *AB* is available to Friday. Similarly, the length of the box *OD* denotes the amount of bread available, and if *OC* is allocated to Crusoe, then *DC* is available to Friday. It follows that any point in the box represents a particular allocation of the two commodities between the two consumers. A point in the centre (*X*) shows a perfectly equal allocation. The point *Y* can be regarded as the imperialist outcome: Crusoe is pushy and commandeers most of both commodities for himself. The point *O* is a possible outcome if Crusoe is too pushy: Friday disposes of the domineering intruder and has all the bread and wine to himself!

The next step is to question which of the various possible commodity divisions is most efficient. To do this requires some information about the preferences of the consumers, since a commodity distribution is clearly inefficient if it does not accord in some way with consumers relative preferences. (If I like coffee and you like tea, but the system results in me getting tea and you getting coffee, then it is a pretty poor system!)

The usual analytical device for studying consumer preferences is the *indifference curve technique*. The essence of indifference curves is quite simple: they are lines connecting combinations of commodities between which the consumer is indifferent in the sense of not preferring one combination to the other. In effect, each indifference curve shows combinations of commodities which yield the consumer the same level of satisfaction. A set of such curves is shown in *Figure 2.3*.

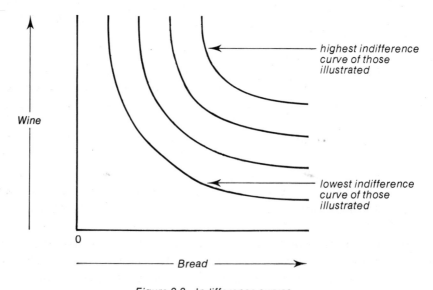

Figure 2.3   Indifference curves

Different indifference curves represent different levels of consumer satisfaction. It is technically incorrect to label the curves according to the quantity or level of satisfaction indicated: we can only say one indifference curve shows a higher level of satisfaction than another, not *how much* higher. Formally this means that indifference curves are *ordinal*, not cardinal, measures of consumer satisfaction. The consumer is assumed to be able to rank his or her preferences as between different combinations of goods but not to be able to specify the absolute amount of satisfaction derived from each combination.

Each indifference curve will be downward sloping to the right so long as the consumer derives satisfaction from consuming additional units of both commodities. The slope of the curves will depend on the relative satisfaction derived from additional units of each commodity. More formally, we can say that the amount of satisfaction derived from one additional unit of any one commodity is known as the *marginal utility*, and that the slope of an indifference curve depends on the relative magnitude of the marginal utility of the commodities in question.

Indifference curves are normally shown as convex to the origin because the more of one commodity a consumer has the more he or she will be prepared to give up in order to obtain an additional unit of another commodity. This phenomenon is related to (but not wholly dependent on) the so-called law of diminishing marginal utility, which says that each additional unit of a commodity consumed in a particular time period confers less utility to the consumer than preceding units. If this tendency is operative for all commodities under consideration, then indifference curves showing a consumer's preferences for any pair of commodities will be convex to the origin.

However, it should be noted that indifference curves are not *necessarily* downward sloping to the right and convex to the origin. This will not be the case in the circumstance where the consumer has so much of particular commodities that he or she becomes satiated. Such a situation is illustrated in *Figure 2.4*. Up to a certain level, additional units of each commodity add to the consumer's satisfaction and hence take him or her on to a higher indifference curve. But, beyond that point (*OA* in the case of wine and *OB* in the case of bread) additional units confer disutility rather than utility. In these circumstances the indifference curves slope upwards to the right, showing that increases in the amounts of any one commodity leave the consumer on the same indifference curve only if he or she is compensated by having more of the other commodity too. When wine consumption is in excess of *OA* and bread consumption in excess of *OB*, the indifference curves actually become concave to the origin: in this case both commodities confer disutility. Thus, if we connect the vertical and horizontal points of the indifference map with dotted lines as in *Figure 2.4*, we have four possibilities. For commodity combinations in the segment *AEB* the consumer has a positive preference for both commodities: in area *AED* he or she has a positive preference for bread but would actually prefer less wine (drowning from the inside out?): in area *BEC* he or she has a positive preference for wine but a negative preference for bread and, finally, in area *CED* he or she has a negative preference for both commodities.

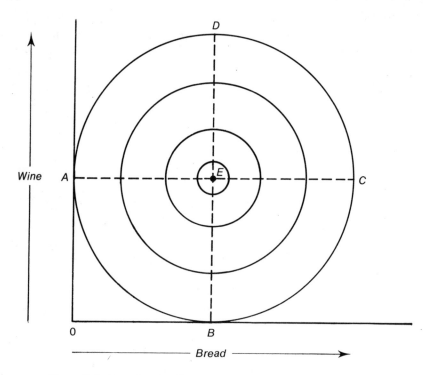

Figure 2.4   Complete indifference curves and the 'effective region'

Economists have typically ignored this possibility of commodities conferring disutility, and have concentrated only on the so-called 'effective region' of consumption (the segment *OAEB* in *Figure 2.4*). Walsh comments that while this may have been reasonable at the time when the indifference curve analysis was developed, it is not longer so.[1] Of course, scarcity is not everywhere abolished (far from it!), but many people in the economically affluent countries are coming to realise that additions to material wealth are not necessarily

[1] V. C. Walsh, *Introduction to Contemporary Microeconomics*, New York, McGraw-Hill, 1970, p. 57.

desirable, especially if the production and consumption of more commodities means more pollution, congestion and environmental destruction. Many young people in particular are starting to question in their own lives the values of material accumulation over and above the minimum requirements of food, clothing and shelter. Economists have been generally rather slow to catch up with these realities, and the continued emphasis on the 'effective region' in indifference curve analysis has been held up as an example of the in-built conservatism of the discipline.

Having briefly considered the principal properties of indifference curves we can now return to the main theme. We are concerned with the evaluation of alternative commodity allocations in a two-person community. We have seen that such evaluation requires knowledge of consumer preferences. We now have a technique for representing such preferences, the indifference curve technique. So let us now superimpose indifference curves on the Edgeworth box diagram in order to assess how differences in consumer preferences determine the optimal pattern of commodity allocation.

Consider *Figure 2.5*. This shows two sets of indifference curves in the Edgeworth box. The curves C_1, C_2, C_3 and C_4 are some of Crusoe's indifference curves: the curves F_1, F_2, F_3 and F_4 are some of Friday's indifference curves. The latter are inverted relative to the former, since points on the top right hand corner will give high levels of satisfaction to Crusoe and low levels of satisfaction to Friday, while points in the bottom left hand corner will give low levels of satisfaction to Crusoe but high levels of satisfaction to Friday.

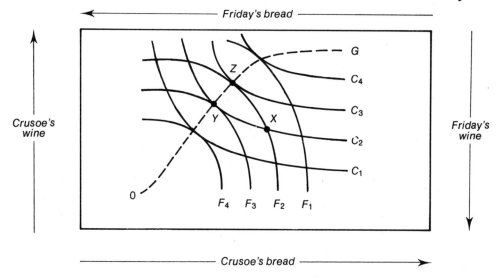

Figure 2.5 Edgeworth box analysis of distributional efficiency

Consider now the equal allocation as indicated in *Figure 2.5* by point X: Crusoe derives a level of satisfaction indicated by C_2 and Friday derives a level of satisfaction indicated by F_2. Is this an efficient as well as equitable outcome? No. The centre of box allocation is inefficient in that other allocations would allow either consumer to move to a higher indifference curve without pushing the other into a lower one. For example, if the allocation was at point Z, Crusoe would attain indifference curve C_3 which lies above C_2, the level of satisfaction given by a centre of box allocation. Friday would still attain indifference curve F_2. Z is efficient in that one consumer cannot attain a higher indifference curve without pushing the other consumer on to a lower indifference curve. This situation satisfies the criterion of ideal allocation that no consumer can be made better off without another being made worse off. The point Y also satisfies this condition. In fact, all points of tangency between the two consumers' indifference curves in the Edgeworth box do so.

Joining these points of tangency gives us a locus of efficient allocations, as shown by the dotted line OG in *Figure 2.5*. This curve is known as the *conflict (or contract) curve* and may take any shape depending on the nature of the particular pair of indifference maps under consideration. In our example its shape is due to the relative strength of Crusoe's preference for wine (causing his indifference curves to be fairly 'flat') and the strength of Friday's preference for bread (causing his indifference curves to be fairly 'steep'). Friday is obviously hungrier whereas Crusoe reveals a more well developed taste for the firewater!

The Price System and Distributional Efficiency

Having dealt with the more technical steps of the orthodox analysis we are in a position to undertake some more interesting interpretation. In particular, we are in a position to evaluate the efficiency of a market economy as a means of distributing commodities between consumers. Orthodox theory is quite clear on this point: the market system is distributionally efficient because it ensures that the allocation will be at some point on the conflict curve and thus in accord with differences in consumers' preferences. Why is this so?

The argument runs as follows. If the allocation is at some point off the conflict curve, both consumers can gain through exchange of commodities. For example, if it was at some point like X, Crusoe would wish to swap bread for wine and Friday would wish to swap wine for bread. Both stand to gain from mutual exchange. Therefore some bartering will occur, and a price system will develop. In order to facilitate exchange it is likely that one commodity will adopt the function of money. But even if exchange is of the simple barter type, a set of implicit prices must exist, for example, two loaves of bread equals one flagon of wine.

Diagrammatically, we can represent the commodity prices in the two-commodity case in terms of a *budget line*. This shows the various combinations of commodities which can be purchased given the consumer's income (or, in the case of the Crusoe-Friday example, his initial stock of the two commodities). For example, the budget line *BD* in *Figure 2.6* shows the case where the consumer could obtain *OB* wine if he or she spent all his or her income on wine, *OD* bread if he or she spent all his or her income on bread, or some intermediate combination such as *OA* wine plus *OC* bread if he or she divided his or her income between the two. The slope of the budget line reflects relative prices. Thus, if bread was to become twice as expensive as before, the budget line would move to the position *OE*, since the consumer could now only obtain half as much bread as before with his or her given income.

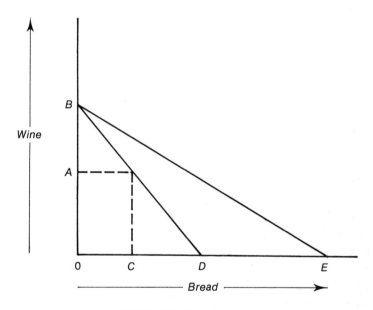

Figure 2.6 Budget lines

The consumer is assumed to maximise his or her utility subject to this budget constraint. Thus, the equilibrium will be at that point where the budget line touches the highest possible indifference curve. Such an equilibrium is shown in *Figure 2.7*. Commodity combinations on indifference curve 3 are unobtainable because the consumers income limits him to combinations bounded by the budget line *CF*. Combinations such as *OA* wine plus *OE* bread are obtainable but give less satisfaction than the combination of *OB* wine plus *OD* bread. This last combination is the ideal from the consumer's viewpoint,

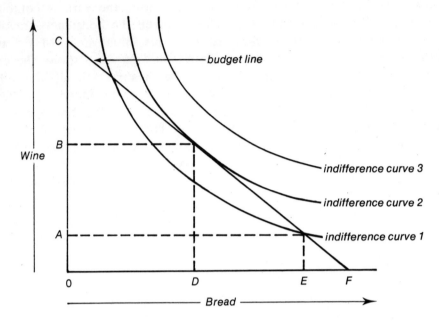

Figure 2.7 Consumer's equilibrium

since it enables him or her to attain the highest possible indifference curve.

In the Crusoe-Friday situation, both consumers will strive to reach such an equilibrium. They will do so by exchanging commodities, and thereby developing a price system. Crusoe seeks to exchange commodities until:

$$\frac{\text{Crusoe's marginal utility of bread}}{\text{Crusoe's marginal utility of wine}} = \frac{\text{price of bread}}{\text{price of wine}}$$

The left hand term is the slope of the indifference curve (known as the marginal rate of substitution) and the right hand term the slope of the budget line (neglecting signs). When the two slopes coincide a tangency point is reached and equilibrium is established. Friday seeks a similar equilibrium where his ratio of marginal utilities equals the price ratio. Given that both consumers face the same commodity prices, then the final outcome will be where:

$$\frac{\text{Crusoe's marginal utility of bread}}{\text{Crusoe's marginal utility of wine}} = \frac{\text{Friday's marginal utility of bread}}{\text{Friday's marginal utility of wine}}$$

The left hand term is the slope of Crusoe's indifference curve and the right hand term is the slope of Friday's (neglecting signs). Where they are equal denotes an allocation at some point on the conflict curve. When this situation is reached, no further voluntary exchange will occur since *both* consumers cannot gain by it. Of course, one can still move to a higher indifference curve but only at the expense of pushing the other onto a lower indifference curve: if the society is characterised by violence such redistributions will occur (theft, of course, comes in this category) but otherwise this cannot be so. We can only say that when the allocation is at some point on the conflict curve, there is no further incentive for exchange to occur: each consumer's marginal rate of substitution is equal to the commodity price ratio. In other words, the rate at which each consumer would be prepared to substitute one commodity for the other is equal to the rate at which such substitution would have to occur. This is said to be an ideal allocation.

The next step is to generalise from this simple two-person two-commodity example to multiple-person multiple-commodity market economies. The same principles are usually held to prevail. Thus, the orthodox argument about the distributional efficiency of the price system can be summarised as follows:

(1) equal distribution of commodities between consumers does not lead to distributional efficiency if consumers tastes differ significantly from each other;

(2) a price system will ensure that the marginal rate of substitution between any pair of commodities is equal for all consumers;

(3) the resulting allocation of commodities between consumers is ideal in that no one consumer can be made better off without another being made worse off.

This sounds very impressive. Let us now look at how impressive it really is. We proceed in two stages: first, an examination of the assumptions underlying the orthodox analysis and, second, an examination of the bias introduced because of the neglect of equity criteria.

Underlying Assumptions

All theories are based on assumptions. Finding real-world examples which do not fit in with the generalisations on which a particular theory is based does not invalidate the theory. However, as pointed out in Chapter 1, it is important that the assumptions not be *systematically* at odds with observed reality. Otherwise the theory distracts attention from the world, rather than helping us to 'act in it intelligently and effectively'.

The orthodox economic analysis that we have been looking at in this chapter is rooted in what is known as the Paretian tradition (after the Italian sociologist and economist Vilfredo Pareto). Some early writers in this tradition sought to deny that their work was based on value-judgements. However, it is impossible to evaluate alternatives without some normative standards. (What is good? How can one allocation be identified as better or worse than another?).

The Paretian value-judgements provide such a normative standard: they provide a basis by which we can rule out particular allocations as 'inferior' to others. The first four assumptions considered here are in this Paretian tradition, and they underly much so-called positive economics as well as the normative analysis of distributional efficiency. As such, an appraisal of them is of very general importance in the understanding of economic orthodoxy.

Assumption 1   The concern is with the welfare of individuals who have independently formulated preferences.

As has often been pointed out, this judgement embodies an individualistic ethic which is in some contrast to the collectivist ethic on which socialist societies are based. To base the economic analysis on the individualistic ethic is to bias it towards a particular type of social system. This is objectionable if the analysis is then used to generate theorems which 'prove' the superiority of one particular type of social system. In effect, the conclusions are built into the assumptions.

A related point concerns the way in which individual objectives and tastes are formulated. Orthodox economics would seem to assume that consumers' preferences are determined quite independently of the economic system, God-given in effect. This has been justifiably described as 'the immaculate conception of the indifference curve'.[2] It is quite misleading. The genetic component in tastes is small relative to the environmental component. Apart from basic needs for food and warmth, most of our preferences are *learned*. This learning process is a very complex one, but consists in part at least of a process of adjustment to the consumption patterns of the society in which one grows up. Indeed, there would appear to be an important stabilising mechanism in that what is seen as desirable is partly determined by what is currently available. In these circumstances we cannot consider preferences to be formulated independently of the existing economic and social order. To build theories on the assumption of independence is at best not helpful in that it diverts attention away from important questions relating to the process of preference formation. At worst, it is positively misleading because the resulting theories tend to bestow an unwarranted legitimacy on the *status quo*.

The more one considers the way in which preferences are formulated, the more one finds problems with the orthodox analysis. A particularly troublesome matter is that of interdependence between preferences and commodity prices. The orthodox theory is based on the assumption that changes in price have no effect on the pattern of consumer preferences. If the indifference curves change position every time prices change then the analysis is incapable of yielding determinate solutions. This is a very real difficulty because it is

---

[2] K. Boulding, *Economics as a Science,* New York, McGraw-Hill, 1970, p. 118.

clear that prices do influence tastes in real-world consumer behaviour. Economics students always delight in putting forward examples of shops which have cleared their shelves of slow-moving items, not by cutting prices as orthodox theory suggests, but by raising them. These are instances of a change in price causing a change in tastes. Any theorem which rests on indifference curve analysis must break down in such cases since independence between tastes and prices is a fundamental requirement in the model. But interdependence exists whenever prices are used by consumers as an indication of quality. (Think about your own consumption decisions and you'll realise how frequently such circumstances arise.)

Assumption 2   Every individual is the best judge of his or her own welfare.

This would appear to be generally a reasonable assumption. However, two provisos are warranted. Firstly, there is the problem associated with non-foreseeable consequences of particular forms of consumption. Many people who start consumption of alcohol, cigarettes and so on, eventually regret it when they realise the full consequences of their decision. In such circumstances the expected utility from a particular course of action and the realised utility may be quite different. Secondly, there is the problem associated with biased information. Rational consumer decision-making requires full information about the range of goods and services available, their attributes and their relative prices. Such circumstances are hard to find in practice. Of course, it is true that there is a great volume of information flow about goods and services in the modern capitalist economy, but much advertising seeks to dupe the potential consumer rather than inform him or her. It is at least debatable whether consumers can be expected to act in an objectively rational manner in circumstances where most of their information is systematically biased. We may conclude that, while the assumption of consumers being the best judge of their own welfare is generally not unreasonable, there are important reasons to doubt its generality when applied to complex capitalist economies.

Assumption 3   Any one individual's welfare depends only on his or her own consumption of marketable goods and is unaffected by non-economic considerations or by the consumption of other individuals.

The main problem here relates to the neglect of 'external effects' of consumption activities. Such effects exist whenever one person's consumption activities affect the welfare of another person. The Edgeworth box analysis disregards such matters; it assumes that Crusoe's satisfaction from his possessions is not affected by how many possessions Friday has, and Friday's satisfaction from his possessions is not affected by how many possessions Crusoe has. In a society characterised by social emulation ('keeping up with the Joneses') this lacks credibility. The importance of 'conspicuous' consumption in consumer be-haviour has long been recognised.[3] If you purchase a brand-new Cadillac car, the pleasure your neighbours get from owning their old cars may well be undermined, and if they respond by buying new Cadillacs too, your satis-faction may be reduced. You may argue that you personally are not so sense-less as to act in this way, but few would deny that the process of the 'keeping up with the Joneses' is of widespread importance. The outcome is that we cannot be confident that each individual seeking to better his lot will increase the welfare of society as a whole—quite an indictment of all social organisa-tions based on individual self-interest![4]

Consider now a rather different type of interdependence: that associated with external effects of consumption which manifest themselves in more physical forms. Take, for example, the case where adverse 'spillover' effects result from proximity of consumers with different tastes. If I go to a cinema alone and smoke I may obtain a certain satisfaction from the whole performance. If you go alone and eat popcorn you may derive a similar pleasure. But, if we both go and sit together, it is unlikely that our satisfaction will be as high, because unpleasant odours will be wafting up your nose and distracting noises will be assailing my ears. (There may, of course, be beneficial 'spillovers' where consumers with similar tastes get together: at least one would deduce this to be the case from the action at 'drive-in' cinemas!)

In the light of these observations, it can be plausibly argued that inter-dependence is much more the typical situation than the independence which orthodox economics assumes. As Boulding says, 'selfishness, or indifference to the welfare of others, is a knife-edge between benevolence on the one side and malevolence on the other. It is something that is very rare.'[5]

Assumption 4 If any change in the allocation of resources increases the welfare of at least one individual without reducing the welfare of any other individual, this change can be considered to have increased social welfare.

This value-judgement is the most characteristic of the Paretian approach, and it is sometimes known as *the* Pareto criterion. It sounds pretty reasonable. Indeed, it has been sometimes said that the wide acceptance of this criterion by economists is due to its totally unobjectionable nature. However, it *is* objectionable in that it begs certain questions. As such, any analysis based on

---

[3] See T. Veblen, *The Theory of the Leisure Class*, London, Unwin Books, 1970, especially Ch. 4.

[4] For an analysis of the effects of these sorts of interdependence see H. Leibenstein, Band-wagon, Snob and Veblen Effects in the Theory of Consumers Demand, *The Quarterly Journal of Economics*, May, 1950, pp. 183-207.

[5] K. Boulding, *Economics as a Science,* New York, McGraw-Hill, 1970, p. 126.

it—such as the proof of the distributional efficiency of price systems—is open to further criticism.

Firstly, it may be noted that there are certain circumstances which satisfy the Pareto criterion but which are not normally acceptable on ethical grounds. Mishan provides an interesting example of a 'mutually beneficial agreement between a shopkeeper and a gang of toughs whereby the latter discontinues its practice of breaking the shopkeeper's windows in exchange for a regular tribute'.[6] Sure, such examples where Pareto optimality conflicts with general standards of ethics may be relatively rare, but for a rule whose main strength purports to be its generality the effect is damaging.

Of more general importance is the observation that the Pareto criterion is applicable to relatively few social circumstances. Most changes in resource allocation in the economy involve *conflict*: some consumers (or groups of consumers) gain while others lose. In these circumstances, the Pareto criterion cannot indicate whether the change is socially desirable or not. What relevance can such a criterion have for a class-stratified society in which conflicting interests are the rule rather than the exception? This is indeed a problem. It has led some economists to seek to formulate more general criteria to deal with such situations.[7] The general theme is one of 'compensation'. It is argued that whether or not a social change is desirable depends on whether the gainers can compensate the losers for their loss in welfare and still be better off than before; and/or whether the losers can bribe the potential winners to refrain from the action. There are many variants of this sort of approach. However, all compensation criteria are dogged by the problem of income distribution and its effects on ability to pay compensation or bribes. As such, compensation criteria have an in-built bias towards the *status quo* and must be rejected by social scientists seeking to study the determinants of social welfare, including the distribution of income.

In terms of the Edgeworth box diagram, the Paretian approach limits us to comparing the distributional efficiency of allocations on the conflict curve with those off it. The former are efficient in the Paretian sense: the latter are not. But we cannot compare the desirability of different allocations on the conflict curve, nor the relative desirability of points off it. Thus we are left with a rather open-ended conclusion. An infinite number of commodity allocations satisfy the Pareto criterion of distributional efficiency. Choice between alternatives requires an explicit statement of the trade-off between equity and efficiency goals. In Dobbs' words, 'maximising welfare has to be viewed in

---

[6] E. J. Mishan, The Futility of Pareto-Efficient Distributions, *The American Economic Review*, December 1972, pp. 975-976.

[7] A survey of such efforts is provided by S. K. Nath, *A Reappraisal of Welfare Economics*, London, Routledge & Kegan Paul, 1969, Ch. 5.

terms of a compromise between diverse ends; and to the extent that the ends are imperfectly comparable, the "best" solution in reconciling them cannot be read off from a system of equations'.[8] Thus, optimum resource allocation cannot be identified in terms of the mechanical application of the Pareto criterion.

So much for the principal assumptions on which the Paretian analysis of economic welfare is based. We turn now to two other matters which have more limited importance in terms of Edgeworth box 'proof' of the distributional efficiency of the market economy.

Assumption 5 Consumers preferences are continuous and 'well behaved' around the equilibrium position.

If preferences are not continuous, then indifference curves cannot be drawn. This is a particular problem in the case of consumer durables, where purchases are 'lumpy'. Thus, in *Figure 2.8* the individual's preference map can be shown only as a series of points: to join them up is ludicrous since that

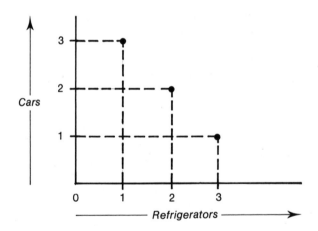

Figure 2.8   Discontinuous preferences

would imply that the consumer would be prepared to sacrifice, say, one-third of a car in order to obtain half a new refrigerator. It is impossible to apply indifference curve analysis in such a situation and any theorem which rests upon that construction becomes accordingly suspect.

[8] M. Dobb, *Welfare Economics and the Economics of Socialism*, Cambs., Cambridge University Press, 1969, p. 253.

Similar problems exist where indifference curves are not convex to the origin; in such circumstances points of tangency between consumers' indifference curves do not necessarily denote a Pareto optimal allocation. However, irksome though these matters are, they are of no great general significance. They constitute a problem with the conventional Edgeworth box analysis, but they can be handled with more complex techniques. They do not substantially undermine the conclusions about the distributional efficiency of the price system in the way that some of the other difficulties with the conventional analysis do.

Assumption 6 No price discrimination.

There is no reason to expect this problem in a Crusoe-Friday economy since there is no third party to discriminate between them in the sale of commodities. But when one generalises the argument to a multiple-person economy, the possibility of such discrimination becomes very real indeed. This is important because, as we shall see, the distributional efficiency of the market breaks down in such circumstances.

Firstly, a definition of price discrimination: charging different prices for the commodity which do not reflect differences in its cost of production and distribution.

Secondly, a consideration of its generality. It takes many forms, such as (i) discrimination between consumers according to sex, race or age (for example in the pricing of bus rides or of any other service where old-age pensioners and/or young children are charged lower prices), (ii) discrimination according to time (for example in the pricing of cinemas offering cut-rate matinees or in the pricing of telephone companies offering 'cheap-rate' calls at a price which does not fully reflect differences in the cost of service provision), (iii) discrimination according to income (for example doctors charging higher fees to wealthier patients than they charge for the same service to poorer patients), and (iv) according to space (for example 'dumping' and other practices where interregional or international price differences cannot be accounted for by differences in costs of supplying each market). Discrimination is a common practice in all conditions where consumers can be separated according to any of these criteria, and where resale of the good or service is not feasible.

Thirdly, we can show that any such discrimination between individuals normally reduces consumer welfare. In *Figure 2.9* we see the case where Crusoe and Friday are forced to pay different prices for the two available commodities (perhaps because some third party has gained control of their supply and wishes to increase his profits by discriminatory pricing). Crusoe's budget line is AE while Friday's is BD. Crusoe will choose the commodity combination at R because his indifference curve C is tangent to his budget line AE, while Friday will choose R because his indifference curve F, is tangent to his budget line BD. However, the ratios of marginal utilities for the two consumers are not equal at that point: R does not lie on the conflict curve. The conclusion, as emphasised by Hidben, is that 'under conditions of price discrimination the distribution of goods in the market must necessarily be inefficient since the two buyers are willing to exchange goods between themselves in order to obtain a higher level of satisfaction'.[9]

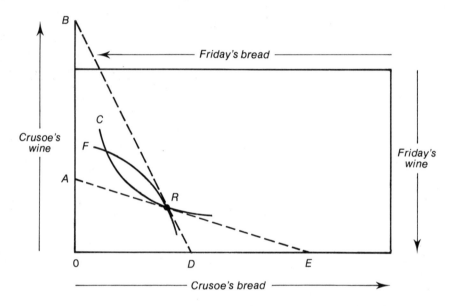

Figure 2.9 Edgeworth box analysis of price discrimination

Equity Considerations

We turn now to a consideration of equity aspects of allocation through the market mechanism. As we have seen, the orthodox analysis of the way in which the price system solves the 'to whom?' allocation problem rests heavily on the Paretian value-judgements. These judgements—the fourth in particular —are efficiency-oriented and ignore equity considerations. But this is not good enough. As Sen puts it, 'an economy can be Pareto optimal and still be perfectly disgusting'.[10] The evaluation of the optimality of resource allocation requires that explicit consideration be taken of equity as well as efficiency criteria.

[9] J. E. Hibden, *Price and Welfare Theory*, New York, McGraw-Hill, 1969, p. 430.
[10] A. K. Sen, *Collective Choice and Social Welfare*, Edinburgh, Oliver & Boyd, 1970, p. 22.

The prime measure of the degree of equity in an economic system is the inequality in the distribution of wealth. This largely determines the inequality in the distribution of power, including purchasing power. The distribution of wealth is the outcome of a complex set of economic, social and political factors. Its evenness varies considerably between different types of societies, but capitalist economies are particularly subject to forces leading to greater inequality. Since such systems are based on material incentives, inequality is a condition for their continued functioning. However, the analytical structure of orthodox economics is not well suited to studying such phenomena. On the contrary, the distribution of wealth is normally taken as determined outside the framework of the analysis. Thus, in the preceding Edgeworth box analysis the initial distribution of bread and wine between Crusoe and Friday was not determined within the model. In this sort of way orthodox economics has diverted attention away from the origins of inequality. This is not to say that orthodox economists have shown no concern for questions of inequality; there has been considerable attention paid to the determination of wage rates paid to different groups of labour, and to the determination of profits rates in different industries. But this is insufficient: a theory of personal income distribution requires a sub-theory of *resource ownership* as well as a sub-theory of *resource prices*. Without knowledge of the resource ownership pattern we cannot say what the distribution of personal income will be, for there are an infinite number of such distributions consistent with any one set of resource prices. Who gets what depends on who owns what, and orthodox economic theory is silent on the latter matter.

Nevertheless, it is clear that there are systematic forces at work which determine the distribution of income and wealth. Differences in capital resources owned constitute the most fundamental source of inequality and determine the class structure of society. It is sometimes contended that such differences are a justifiable reward for diligence and thrift; according to this view inequality is a consequence of the system by which meritorious activity is materially rewarded. There is little substance in the view. Certainly, the wealth of some particular individuals is a direct consequence of their energy in economic matters and their propensity to save, but the general association between wealth and diligence seems rather weak. (Indeed, the role played by diligence and frugality in the accumulation of wealth has been likened to the role played by original sin in theology!) Particularly important is the effect of material inheritance. Even if the original accumulation of wealth could be considered the reward for meritorious activity, this would not itself justify the wealth of the sons and daughters of the meritorious. The inter-generational transfer of wealth is obviously one of the sources of inequality, and its importance as such clearly weakens the argument that the inequality is in some sense a justifiable, or even desirable, phenomenon.

Moreover, it should be noted that inequalities in the distribution of wealth tend to have a cumulative effect, since wealth confers power and puts the wealthy in a more favourable strategic position. One interesting aspect of this can be illustrated in terms of the Edgeworth box diagram. Consider the point X in *Figure 2.10*. This represents an initial wealth allocation where Crusoe owns most of both commodities, and Friday is correspondingly poorly endowed. X is not a stable position in the sense that it is not on the conflict curve, so exchange will normally occur until such a position is reached. The outcome could be anywhere between point Y and point Z. It will be near Y if Friday is the beter negotiator; or near Z if Crusoe strikes the better outcome. Which is more likely? The latter, because Crusoe has more power in the bargaining process. Among other things he is in a position to temporarily withhold his goods from the market, whereas Friday is unlikely to be able to hold out for long because of his greater proximity to the starvation level. All this simply illustrates the general point that wealth confers power and this can be used to further increase the inequality in the distribution of wealth.

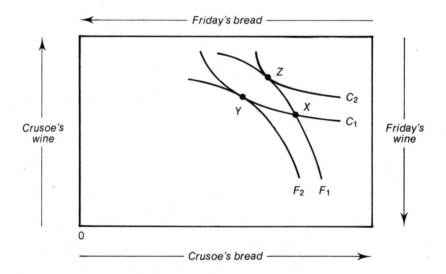

Figure 2.10   Alternative outcomes of the exchange process

It seems appropriate to conclude that while the market economy may get relatively high marks for distributional efficiency (subject to the reservations in the preceding section of this chapter) it is likely to score badly in terms of distributional equity.

Some Implications for Policy Issues

This chapter concludes with some illustrations of the importance of the argument considered in this chapter. Particular attention is paid to the debate on the relative merits of *price* and *rationing* systems of commodity distribution. This controversy provides an example of the distinction between economic analysis and economic dogma. The presumption in favour of price systems, (and, by extension, capitalist rather than socialist organisations) which orthodox economic theory is commonly held to 'prove' turns out to be unsupported by economic analysis.

The price system is, of course, just one means of distributing a given supply of commodities. An alternative, sometimes introduced in wartime, is a rationing system, whereby each consumer is given equal quantities of all available commodities.[11] Such a system is usually regarded as appropriate only in times of national emergency, because the absence of a price system has distorting effects on the allocation process. As Dorfman says 'all systems of rationing . . . get low marks for distributional efficiency'.[12] However, it is quite incorrect to assert that economic theory demonstrates the general superiority of price systems over rationing systems as methods of commodity distribution. The reasons for this are threefold:

Firstly, the use of a rationing system does not necessarily destroy the possibility of prices playing an allocative role. As many commentators note, rationing tends to be accompanied by 'black markets'. This sounds ominous (!) but once the normative implication of the terminology is overcome it can be argued that black markets perform a valuable role. Indeed, it is possible that the combination of rationing plus black market operations is more ideal in some circumstances than the use of a straight price system. What black markets do is to allocate some 'surplus' part of the commodity supply to those consumers with the greatest ability to pay. The result is that all consumers receive a certain minimum allocation of each commodity through the rationing system, and the consumers with special demands for particular commodities augment this with purchases through the black market.[13] Many would consider this preferable to complete reliance on a price system where some consumers may fall below the minimum subsistence requirement in some commodities.

Secondly, the price system is not necessarily more efficient than a rationing

[11] There are various forms of rationing systems. That considered here is the most extreme. Some compromise with the price system can be achieved by using a 'points' system: see, for example, J. E. Hibden, *Price and Welfare Theory*, New York, McGraw-Hill, 1969, pp. 85-89.

[12] R. Dorfman, *Prices and Markets*, Englewood Cliffs, N.J., Prentice-Hall, 1967, p. 114.

[13] Note that there is no reason to suppose that the black-market prices will necessarily be higher than the price that would prevail in a free market situation: see K. Boulding, *Economic Analysis*, Third Edition, London, Hamish Hamilton, 1955, pp. 140-142.

system. In terms of the Edgeworth box analysis, the rationing allocation is the middle of box allocation and, as already noted, this is distributionally inefficient where consumers' tastes are not similar. Only where tastes are similar does the centre-box allocation lie on the conflict curve. However, supplementary black-market systems and exchange between consumers will tend to make the allocation more efficient: as demonstrated in *Figure 2.5* an initial centre-box allocation is likely to be modified through the process of exchange to one nearer the conflict curve. So, if exchange is permitted, a rationing system may not be particularly inefficient.[14] Indeed, most of the accusations about its inefficiency are ill-founded. Boulding provides an example of a popular fallacy in this regard: 'once rationing is extended from commodities where needs are approximately equal, such as sugar, to more complex commodities such as gasoline, clothing, and the like, the system inevitably becomes more and more complicated, with different rations for different classes of people'.[15] He confuses need with demand. Consumers needs for clothing, motor cars, etc. *are* approximately equal. What is not equal is their wealth and hence their effective demand. But to imply, as Boulding does, that rationing systems are less efficient than price systems, is tautological if the distribution achieved by the price system is taken as the ideal! In fact, since we can't deduce needs from actual demand patterns, we cannot be certain that equal allocations are necessarily inefficient in terms of a 'needs' criterion.

As we have already seen in this chapter, price systems are only distributionally efficient under very restrictive assumptions (perfect knowledge, absence of price discrimination, etc.). Since both price and rationing systems can be distributionally inefficient we cannot say on *a priori* grounds which is to be preferred from this viewpoint.

Thirdly, even if the price system is distributionally more efficient than rationing, it will almost certainly result in a less equitable outcome. By definition, the centre-box allocation is the most equitable. However, the price system is most unlikely to result in an equally equitable outcome: it will only do so where the consumers have equal wealth. In all other cases, any possible gain in distributional efficiency is attained by a definite sacrifice of equity. Thus, in *Figure 2.11* the rationing allocation is at *R* while the price system might lead to an outcome such as *S*. In such a case the choice of system obviously depends on the relative weights attached to equity and efficiency consideration.

---

[14] An interesting illustration of this point, and other aspects of rationing systems is provided by R. A. Radford, The Economic Organisation of a POW Camp, *Economica*, Vol. 12, 1945, also reprinted in K. Hancock, B. Hughes and R. Wallace, (Eds.), *Applied Economics: Readings for Australian Students,* Sydney, McGraw-Hill, 1972, pp. 13-20.

[15] K. Boulding, *Economic Analysis,* Third Edition, London, Hamish Hamilton 1955, pp. 139-140.

However, it is also possible that the price system outcome could be at T because as we have already seen, the price system is distributionally efficient only under very restrictive conditions.

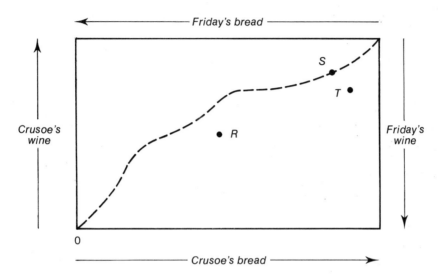

Figure 2.11 Commodity distribution under price and rationing systems

Of course, it is possible that equity may be increased by other means than by replacing the price system by a rationing system: through a more progressive taxation system for example. However, as we will see in Chapter 7, such policies have limited effectiveness in practice. In any case this does not absolve the economist from considering equity considerations. At a minimum there is a responsibility to do as Scitovsky suggests and 'point out the nature of eventual redistributions likely to accompany a given change, and stress the necessity of basing economic policy on considerations both of economic efficiency and social justice'.[16]

Rationing, then, cannot be as lightly dismissed as it usually is as a measure to be used only in wartime or other emergency situations. Its potential applications are very broad, and a great many countries are now using it as a means of allocating services such as health and education. Any 'welfare state' system of allocating these services essentially derives its logic from the theory of

[16] T. Scitovsky, A Note on Welfare Propositions in Economics, *The Review of Economic Studies*, Vol. 9, 1941, pp. 77-88, also reprinted in American Economic Association, *Readings in Welfare Economics*, London, George Allen & Unwin Ltd., 1969, pp. 390-401.

rationing. Since the principle is becoming acceptable in this way, there are strong possibilities that it could be extended to other fields, thus increasing the equity of our economic systems. One argument to beware of, and one which we are now in a position to see as fallacious, is that such 'welfare state' provision is undesirable because it is necessarily inefficient. Such arguments are frequently heard from doctors in countries such as America and Australia where health services have been largely provided privately rather than publicly. However, as we have seen, private provision of goods and services through a price system is not necessarily any more efficient than public provision. Moreover, public provision is generally more equitable. To argue for continued private provision is, in effect, to argue that income should be redistributed to already-wealthy doctors from the poor and sick.

CHAPTER THREE

How?

Most goods can be produced by a variety of different methods. There are limits: even the Bible recognises that 'grapes are not gathered from thorns, or figs from thistles'.[1] Nevertheless, it is the exceptional commodity that cannot be produced with different combinations of productive inputs; and technological progress is constantly enlarging the range of possibilities. Guitars can be hand-made as they have been for centuries in Spain, or they can be mass-produced by mechanised methods as they now are in most industrially developed nations. Even a knowledge of economic theory can be gained by various methods, ranging from reading books to attending lectures or receiving private tutorials. There is a question of choice and, given that society's resources are not infinite, each decision has important repercussions. You may not be a guitar-player and may feel indifferent as to whether guitars are made by labour-intensive or capital-intensive methods. However, if the former alternative is chosen, less labour is available for other uses and this may have adverse effects on other sectors of the economy, in terms of raising costs above the level that would otherwise pertain. Decisions about how productive resources are to be used in different sectors of the economy are interdependent. Therefore, the nature of such decisions is important not only to the individual people concerned with that sector but also to people earning their livelihood in other sectors of the economy. This is especially true because individual decisions on methods of production affect the relative rewards to labour, land and capital inputs and, given unequal ownership of these resources in the community, this helps to determine the distribution of income. Thus, the 'how?' question gains at least part of its importance from its interdependence with the first allocation problem, 'to whom?'.

This chapter is concerned with examining what generally determines the chosen production technique, and whether or not the outcome is in the interests of the community. Clearly, in practice, this choice is a very technical one, often requiring engineering skills of the highest order. However, there are important general economic principles. We begin with an examination of the orthodox economic analysis.

[1] Matthew 7:16.

Techniques for Analysing Productive Efficiency

An economy is endowed with a number of factors of production, conventionally grouped into labour, land and capital (where capital is used in the economists' sense as relating to physical assets such as buildings and machinery, rather than its lay usage as financial assets). A simple model of how any pair of these resources can be combined is shown as *Figure 3.1*. This indicates the amount of labour and land used by different producers in making a given quantity of a similar commodity (say 1,000 loaves of bread per year).

Figure 3.1   Usage of land and labour resources by different producers making the same output

Let us now compare the efficiency of these various producers. As a first step, we can identify the most technically efficient ones as *A, M, K* and *I*. All others are technically inefficient in the sense that they use more labour and/or more land than *A, M, K* and *I* in producing the same output. However, we cannot say which of *A, M, K* and *I* is most efficient: *A* uses more labour than *M* but less land, while *M* uses more labour than *K* but less land, and *K* uses more labour than *I* but less land. We can only say that all are technically efficient. To see which is the most *economically* efficient, we need to introduce information about the relative prices of the land and labour inputs. These relative prices can be represented in the form of *isocost* lines. These are lines joining combinations of inputs which generate the same total cost. A number of such curves are shown in *Figure 3.2*: each represents a different total outlay on inputs, those to the right indicating greater sums than those to the left. The slope is determined by the ratio of the two resource prices: the slope will be steeper the cheaper labour is relative to land because, for a given expenditure, more labour can be purchased the lower the wage rate.

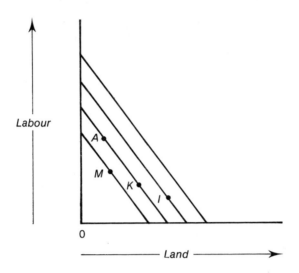

Figure 3.2 Identifying economically efficient production methods by the use of isocost lines

Look now at the four producers *A, M, K* and *I. M* is shown to be the most efficient in its use of inputs because it is on the lowest isocost line. *A* and *K* spend more on land and labour to produce a similar output, while *I* is the least efficient of all.

If, instead of considering a small number of alternative methods of combining inputs in the productive process we consider a very large number, this analysis can be generalised so as to introduce the *isoquant* construct. Isoquants are lines connecting the minimum combinations of inputs which can be used to produce a given level of output. Thus, they show the various *technically* efficient ways in which a particular output can be generated. A set of such curves is shown in *Figure 3.3*.

Each isoquant represents a different level of output, the ones to the right relating to higher outputs than those to the left. The curves are normally downward sloping to the right, because the inputs are at least partially substitutable for each other. If the substitutability were perfect the isoquants would be straight lines: their normal convexity to the origin indicates that as more and more units of one input are used in the production of a given output, the amount of the other input thereby saved declines. This phenomenon is related to the law of diminishing returns which states that, beyond a certain point, adding extra units of one input to a fixed quantity of another input will lead to diminishing additions to the total output.

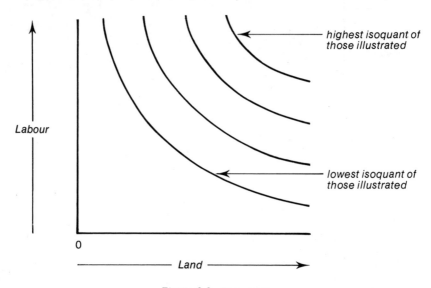

Figure 3.3   Isoquants

The parallels with indifference curve analysis should be fairly obvious. However, there is one important difference. Whereas indifference curves can only be interpreted as an ordinal representation of consumers utility, isoquants are capable of *cardinal* interpretation. Isoquants can be labelled with actual values of output obtainable from different input combinations. Thus, we can not only say that one combination of inputs is capable of producing more output than another combination, but we can actually specify how much more output.

The isocost lines can now be reintroduced in order to identify how any one producer can determine which input combination is most efficient. Assume the producer seeks to minimise the cost of producing a given output (say 1,000 loaves of bread a year). We see in *Figure 3.4* that this can be done in various ways, for example by using *OA* labour and *OF* land, *OB* labour and *OE* land, or *OC* labour and *OD* land. The first of these is the cheapest since it involves the expenditure on inputs indicated by the lowest isocost line. The second involves higher costs, and the third higher still. *OB* labour plus *OE* land is the producer's equilibrium.

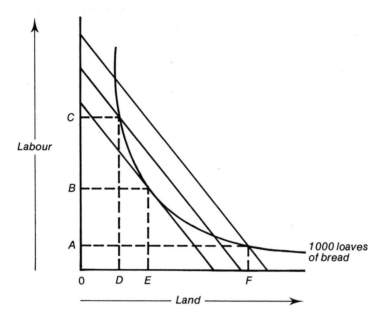

Figure 3.4 Minimising the cost of producing a particular output

More formally we can denote the equilibrium as being established at that position where the ratio of input prices is equal to the ratio of their marginal products, where the *marginal product* of any one input is defined as the addition to total product resulting from the addition of one more unit of the input, the quantity of other inputs remaining constant. In the two input case we can write this as follows:

$$\frac{\text{price of labour}}{\text{price of land}} = \frac{\text{marginal product of labour}}{\text{marginal product of land}}$$

The right hand term is the slope of the isoquant (sometimes known as the marginal rate of technical substitution), and the left hand term is the slope of the isocost line (ignoring signs). When the equality holds, there is no incentive for the producer to change his technique of production, since he is minimising the cost of production for the chosen output level.

We turn now from the individual producer to the economy as a whole, and pose the question of what constitutes an efficient allocation of inputs between producers. For simplicity, we study the two-industry two-input case. This enables us to use a variant on the now familiar Edgeworth box analysis and, since the procedure closely parallels the analysis of distributional efficiency in Chapter 2, we can proceed quite quickly.

Figure 3.5 shows an Edgeworth box with input quantities measured on the axes, the two inputs being labour and land. The width of the box indicates the amount of land available in the community and the height shows the amount of labour available. These two inputs can be used for the production of only two goods, say bread and wine (it may be that these are the two commodities that can be produced, or the only two that the members of the community desire).

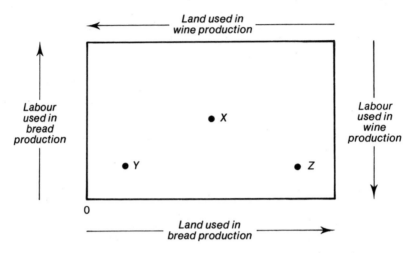

Figure 3.5   Applying the Edgeworth box analysis to the study of production techniques.

Any point in this box indicates a particular allocation of resources to the two different uses. For example, the point X in the centre of the box indicates that the resources are used equally in the two industries. A point such as Y indicates that the majority of both resources are used in wine production (thus providing the prerequisite for a life of debauchery?). A point such as Z indicates that most land is used in bread production, while wine is made by very labour intensive methods.

Suppose the initial allocation is at the centre of the box. Is this an efficient use of resources? To answer this we must introduce some information about the productivity of the inputs in the alternative uses. This is where isoquants come in useful. In *Figure 3.6* W_1, W_2, W_3 and W_4 are some isoquants for wine production, and B_1, B_2, B_3 and B_4 are some isoquants for bread production. The former are inverted relative to the latter since points in the bottom left hand corner will yield high outputs of wine but low outputs of bread, while points in the top right hand corner will lead to much bread but little wine being produced.

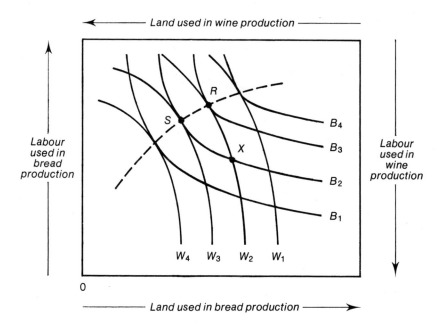

Figure 3.6 Edgeworth box analysis of productive efficiency

The point X at the centre of the box is revealed as inefficient. Such an allocation of resources will lead to the production of two units of bread and two units
of wine. It would be possible to produce more of both commodities with the
same resources. At point R, for example, it is possible to produce two units
of wine and three units of bread. Similarly, at point S, we could have three
units of wine and two of bread. At these points the two isoquants are tangen-
tial, so no further increase in the output of one commodity is possible without
reducing the production of the other commodity. All such points of tangency
can be joined to form the *conflict (or contract) curve*. This is the locus of all
input combinations which are efficient in the sense that no reallocation of
inputs can increase the output of some goods without reducing the output of
others. This curve may take any shape depending on the particular pair of
isoquants under consideration. In our example, its shape is due to the relatively
high productivity of labour in bread production (causing the isoquants to be
fairly 'flat') and the relatively high productivity of land in wine production
(causing the isoquants to be fairly 'steep'). Bread is best produced by labour
intensive methods while wine is best produced by land intensive methods.

The Price System and Productive Efficiency

Most economic textbooks state quite simply that the price system will ensure productive efficiency. The argument is that if the input allocation is at some point off the conflict curve, there is a clear incentive to substitute resources between the different uses. It pays, because the output of *both* bread and wine can be increased. Thus, bread and wine producers can be expected to seek to exchange inputs until a point on the conflict curve is reached. This results in the formation of markets for the inputs and the development of a resource price system. Each producer will continue trading until an allocation on the conflict curve is reached, but then voluntary trading will cease since at that stage each producer can only improve his position at the expense of the other.

As we have seen, each producer will attain equilibrium where the ratio of marginal products between inputs (or marginal rate of technical substitution) is equal to the ratio of the input prices. Given that both producers face the same input prices, then:

$$\frac{\text{marginal product of labour in bread production}}{\text{marginal product of land in bread production}} = \frac{\text{marginal product of labour in wine production}}{\text{marginal product of land in wine production}}$$

The left hand side of this equation is the slope of the bread isoquant: the right hand side is the slope of the wine isoquant (ignoring signs). The equality indicates a point of tangency such as found only on the conflict curve. In this way the price system is said to achieve productive efficiency.

Thus the usual set of conclusions mirrors very closely the one previously established in relation to efficiency in distribution:

(1)   employing resources in the same proportion in each industry does not lead to productive efficiency if their relative productivity differs between industries;

(2)   an ideal price system will ensure that the marginal rate of technical substitution between any pair of inputs is equal for all producers;

(3)   the resulting allocation of inputs between industries is efficient in that the output of one industry cannot be increased without reducing the output of the other.

Underlying Assumptions

Let us now retrace some steps and have a closer look at the analysis of productive efficiency under a price system. Like the supposed demonstration of the distributional efficiency of the price system, the analysis of productive efficiency rests on some rather restrictive assumptions. Most obviously, it is clearly in the Paretian tradition, the peculiar characteristics of which we have already examined in some detail. The principal criterion of Pareto optimality is actually quite reasonable when applied to the analysis of production decisions: no-one would deny that an allocation of inputs between industries was inefficient if it were possible to redistribute them so as to increase the output of both industries. It does leave open the question of how one compares the efficiency of two allocations neither of which is on the conflict curve, and how one compares the desirability of two points on the conflict curve. But, as far as it goes, it is generally a quite unobjectionable proposition.

The problems lie rather with some of the ancillary assumptions which appear systematically at odds with many characteristics of modern capitalism. The following are some of the most important aspects.

Assumption 1   All producers have perfect knowledge of input prices and productivities and, on the basis of this information, minimise costs of producing any given output.

The first part of this proposition is possibly more acceptable than the corresponding assumption about consumers having perfect knowledge about commodity prices and attributes. A considerable amount of business activity goes into generating information about the prices and productivity of different inputs. However, to assume such knowledge to be perfect is not generally tenable. Indeed, even taking account of the fact that information is often quite costly to obtain, there seems to be a systematic tendency for this information to be insufficient for rational decision-making. Many producers are not aware of the availability of all resources and their prices and productivities. In particular, they may not regularly scrutinise the latest technical developments and assess their implications for the selection of production techniques within their firm. Cyert and March[2] emphasise this point in their analysis of the behaviour of individual firms: information is generated by search activity which usually occurs only in response to a problem situation. In these circumstances we must have somewhat diminished confidence in the conclusions derived from a model which sees firms continually seeking the information necessary for adjustment of production techniques so as to ensure equality between input productivity and resource price ratios.

Similar remarks may be made about the assumption of cost minimisation. Of course, the minimisation of costs involved in the production of any output

[2] R. M. Cyert & J. G. March, *A Behavioral Theory of the Firm*, Englewood Cliffs N.J., Prentice-Hall, 1963.

is a necessary part of the more general objective of profit maximisation. While this seems to be a generally plausible hypothesis about business behaviour, some economists have doubt about its applicability to large organisations where managerial objectives are not the same as the objectives of the owners. Williamson[3], for example, has argued strongly that, where scope for managerial discretion exists, it will frequently lead to decisions being taken to raise costs above the minimum necessary level. Excess costs are seen as a purposeful rather than accidental outcome, since managers derive personal benefits from expenditures on such things as additional staff and emoluments in the form of free cars, thick-pile carpets, expense-account entertainment and so on. Whether or not Williamson's model provides a useful general analysis is open to question but, to the extent that firms have imperfect knowledge and/or engage in wasteful expenditure, there is some doubt about the usefulness of cost minimisation as a general rule of business conduct. This being so the assertion that resource allocation under a free enterprise system will be efficient also loses some of its generality.

Assumption 2   No external economies or diseconomies of production.

Attempts by one producer to increase the level of output produced may increase the costs of production incurred by other producers. This is quite a likely outcome, because the first producer's expansion will increase the demand for the various productive inputs used, and any resulting increase in input prices will affect all producers. An external diseconomy of production can be said to exist, because the expansion of one producer's output has adverse spillover effects on other sectors of the economy.

External economies can also exist; this is where one producer's increase in output leads to a decrease in the costs of other producers. An example would be in a geographically remote district dependent on a single industry such as mining: only when that industry had grown to a certain size and established the transport and other infrastructure necessary to serve it would it become profitable for other industries to move in. The expansion of the first industry is said to generate external economies, because it has beneficial spillovers on other sectors of the economy.

These external effects associated with changes in the volume of production cause systematic resource misallocation. In a market economy characterised by external effects, the prices paid for inputs by any one producer do not reflect the cost to the community as a whole: the private costs will exceed the social costs where external economies exist, and the social costs will

---

[3] O. E. Williamson, *The Economics of Discretionary Behaviour*, Englewood Cliffs N.J., Prentice-Hall, 1964.

exceed the private costs where external diseconomies exist. Hence, the selection of production techniques on the basis of private costs is likely to systematically conflict with the minimisation of social costs for the economy as a whole. In particular, there tends to be a bias towards the use of an environmentally-destructive technology because producers do not normally have to pay a price for their spoilation of air and water resources.

Assumption 3   All resources are perfectly mobile between alternative uses.

Resources must be used where their productivity is highest for us to be able to conclude that the operation of a price system is conducive to productive efficiency. But in practice, resources are often geographically and/or occupationally immobile. The reasons for this are many and varied, and we will return to this issue again in Chapter 5. However, it should be clear that resource immobility is sufficiently widespread to cast serious doubt on the conclusions of an argument which is based on the assumption of perfect mobility.

Assumption 4   The productivity of resources in alternative uses is determined independently of the pattern of resource prices.

This assumption is necessary for the use of the isoquant/isocost analysis. If it does not hold, then changes in the position of isocosts (reflecting changes in input prices) will change the productivity of inputs and, hence, the position of the isoquants. In such a situation the producer's equilibrium is indeterminate. In fact, independence of resource prices and productivities is quite a reasonable assumption so long as the analysis is confined to a very short time period. It is almost certainly more reasonable than the assumption of independence between commodity prices and consumers preferences, which is the analytical parallel. For a given state of technology, the maximum output obtainable from any particular combination of inputs is more or less fixed. The problem is a temporal one. *Technological change* occurs over time, changing the outputs obtainable from different combinations of inputs. Moreover, (and here is the real problem for the orthodox analysis), the form of technological change depends on input *prices*, among other things. Thus, if land is cheap relative to labour, technological change will tend to be labour-saving (isoquants shift from *AB* to *AC* in *Figure 3.7*). On the other hand, if land is the relatively expensive input, technological change will tend to be land-saving (as represented by a shift to *BD*).

What this means is that input prices and productivities are not independent when the possibility of technological change is introduced. Yet the Edgeworth box 'proof' of the productive efficiency of the price system requires such independence. As such, the proof is not applicable in dynamic situations.

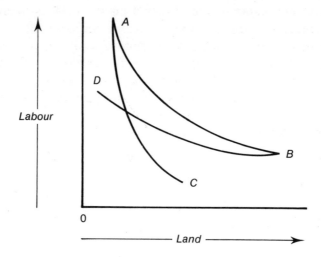

Figure 3.7   Isoquants illustrating biased technological change

Assumption 5   Physical relationships between inputs and outputs are continuous and 'well behaved' around the equilibrium position.

Technically, this means that the production possibilities can be depicted as smooth isoquants which are convex to the origin. This will not happen if there are indivisibilities in the productive process such that labour, land and capital inputs can only be combined in discrete units. In practice, capital (and, to a lesser extent, land) tends to be 'lumpy'. A steel manufacturing firm can have one blast furnace or two, but it is difficult to attach any meaning to intermediate numbers. This denies the possibility of constructing isoquants, in the same way that commodity indivisibilities render impossible the construction of indifference curves. (Look back to *Figure 2.8*). The result is not that the theorem of productive efficiency becomes necessarily invalid: rather it is not demonstrable by the usual method. A similar point relates to other technical difficulties with the orthodox analysis, for example the problems raised by isoquants which are not always convex to the origin. Such matters require the use of more complex analytical techniques, but do not substantially change the general conclusions to be drawn.

Assumption 6   No price discrimination.

The foregoing analysis of productive efficiency rests on the assumption that all buyers of resources pay the same prices; absence of such unique resource prices would mean that we could not be sure of attaining some resource distribution on the conflict curve. Exactly the same argument used earlier in relation to price discrimination in goods markets (see *Figure 2.9* and the associated section of the text) applies again. Such discrimination applied in input markets will normally reduce output below attainable levels, since it destroys the proportionality between input productivity and input prices.

This completes our examination of the assumptions. If it has been tedious it is because there are so many loopholes in the orthodox analysis. Of course, every model must be based on simplifying assumptions, but it appears that the neo-classical analysis is based on some particularly problematic ones.

Equity Considerations

The foregoing analysis is concerned exclusively with efficiency considerations and says nothing about any of the other criteria for appraising economic and social systems. Equity considerations for example, are not explicitly considered in this analysis. However, they are implicit in it. What do we see when we make them explicit?

This requires that we examine rather more carefully the way in which input prices are determined. The orthodox theory treats this matter quite simply. In Lipsey's words 'The traditional theory of distribution states that distribution is simply a special case of price theory. The income of any factor of production (and hence the amount of the national product that it is able to command) depends on the price that is paid for the factor and the amount that is used. If we wish to build up a theory of distribution we thus need a theory of factor prices.'[4] The demand for each input is seen to vary according to its physical productivity in different uses; the higher the productivity the more is demanded. It also depends on the price obtained for the finished product that it helps to produce; the higher the price of the finished product, the higher the demand for inputs. It is in this latter sense that the demand for inputs is described as a *derived* demand; it is derived from the consumers' demand for the output of the production process.

Inputs, as we have seen, are conventionally grouped into labour, land and capital. The supply of each is partly determined by physical factors (particularly important in the case of land), partly by social factors (for example community attitudes towards the appropriate length of the working week and the status associated with different types of employment), and partly by the market price. Generally speaking, for each type of employment, input supply and input prices are taken to be positively associated: the higher the price the higher the supply and vice versa. Putting demand and supply considerations together the actual pattern of input prices is determined. The equilibrium price for each input is that at which demand equals supply.

[4] R. G. Lipsey, *An Introduction to Positive Economics*, Third Edition, London, Weidenfeld and Nicolson, 1970, p. 329.

This is a very simplified outline of what is sometimes known as *marginal productivity theory*. Historically, it has been used to legitimise income inequality in capitalist systems on the grounds that it shows that the pattern of rewards reflects the productivity of different inputs and, by implication, the effort expended.[5] Of course, this is sheer nonsense. The association between productivity and input prices is clear only for the last unit of each input employed: for all other units the value of marginal product exceeds the input price. The input prices also depend on other things than productivity, such as the degree of monopoly which resource buyers are able to develop. And, most importantly, an ethical justification of inequality in the distribution of income would have to concern itself with the pattern of resource *ownership* as well as the pattern of resource *prices*: who gets what depends on who owns what!

One interesting aspect of this can be illustrated in terms of the Edgeworth box analysis. This concerns the interdependence between the pattern of consumers' demand and the relative prices of different inputs. The pattern of consumers' demand depends, among other things, on the distribution of income; but it also plays a major role in determining input prices and, hence, the distribution of income. Consider the alternative resource allocations depicted in *Figure 3.8*. If the resources are allocated as at point Z the implied resource price ratio (OB/OD) is different from that implied by a resource allocation at point Y (OA/OC). This is important, given that the resources of the community are not owned equally by all. The private ownership of resources that accompanies the price system under capitalist organisation invariably results in such unequal holdings: some own nothing but labour, whereas others own land and capital. The relative factor prices therefore determine the distribution of income. In practice, the distribution is always skewed and it is important to put these equity considerations against the alleged efficiency advantages in any appraisal of the effects of the price system.

But we can go further than this. There are more fundamental problems with the orthodox analysis. Probably the most important concerns the concept of *capital*. As we have seen, the neo-classical theory of distribution relies heavily upon the distinction between labour, land and capital and the possibility of distinguishing between the productivity of each. But this is not as easy as first appears, because capital, as an input, is not easily defined except in terms of its own profitability.

We earlier defined capital in terms of physical inputs in the productive

[5] For example, 'what a social class gets is, under natural law, what it contributes to the general output of industry', J. B. Clark, Distribution is Determined by Rent, *The Quarterly Journal of Economics*, Vol. 5, 1891, p. 313.

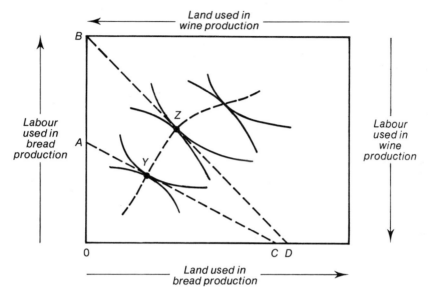

Figure 3.8 Alternative resource price ratios

process, such as buildings and machinery. This is alright at the 'micro' level but how are we to aggregate these items so as to get a measure of the total capital input in the economy? (What is the sum of two blast furnaces, an office block and twelve trucks?) The usual solution is to use a *monetary* measure (the sum of two blast furnaces, an office block and twelve trucks is their total capitalised value). But this is where the problems start. The capitalised value of the assets reflects their profitability.[6] Thus, aggregate capital becomes defined in terms of its own profitability.

The implications of this for the orthodox theory of distribution are considerable. There is a clear element of circularity in the theory because the value of capital depends on the rate of return (profits), while at the same time the value of capital is used to determine the rate of return. Either profits or wage rates must be determined outside the market, in which case factor prices are not a function of productivity, so much as some other social-political-power relations. The eminent British economist Joan Robinson concludes from this that 'the marginal productivity theory is all bosh'.[7] Not all participants in the

---

[6] Chapter 6 explores this matter of asset valuation in more detail.

[7] J. Robinson, Prelude to A Critique of Economic Theory, *Oxford Economic Papers*, Volume 13, 1961, pp. 7-14.

debate agree.[8] However, there is no doubt that the difficulties with the concept of capital further undermine the ability of the neo-classical theory to provide a systematic theoretical rationale for the distribution of income in a capitalist economy.

Some Applications to Policy Issues

Like the previous chapter, this one concludes with some brief comments on applications of the analysis. Particular emphasis is put on the capitalism versus socialism debate since the Edgeworth box analysis of production (and argument derived from it) is sometimes held to provide an intellectual rationale for the capitalistic means of allocating resources between different uses. Only when the price system is allowed to serve as the allocator between different uses, it is said, can economic efficiency be guaranteed. Conversely, the problem with socialist organisation is that there is no explicit price mechanism to ensure that economic inefficiencies are avoided. It is argued that socialist planners cannot be aware of the many variations in resource productivities and, hence, are less able than hard-headed profit-maximising capitalists to select the most efficient resource combination for the production of a given output of a particular commodity.

This pro-capitalist argument is backed up by well-known cases of technological blunders in socialist-based countries. In the Soviet Union, for example, there have been well-publicised cases where inappropriate technology has been used, involving the use of production methods which were much too large-scale and capital intensive relative to the market size and labour and capital available. Similarly, in the People's Republic of China, western commentators have pointed to the attempts to establish small-scale steel production units in the communes during the period known as 'The Great Leap Forward'; here the problem was said to arise from the neglect of scale economies and the lack of technical expertise. Capitalist economists argue that such mistakes are a problem which can be avoided by the use of a price mechanism, which effectively translates capital and labour availability into terms on which the self-interested producer can base a rational decision.

Of course, this argument has a certain credibility about it. The selection of production techniques is a great problem in socialist economies, especially centralist ones such as the Soviet Union. However, the argument is far from

---

[8] A comprehensive treatment of the arguments is to be found in G. Harcourt, *Some Cambridge Controversies in the Theory of Capital*, Cambs, Cambridge University Press, 1972. Shorter summaries include the introduction to G. C. Harcourt & N. F. Laing (Eds.), *Capital and Growth,* Harmondsworth, Penguin Books, 1971, and E. J. Nell, Property and the Means of Production, *Review of Radical Political Economics*, Summer 1972, pp. 1-27.

a conclusive one in favour of capitalist organisation.

Firstly, it is clear that socialists do not have a monopoly on blunders! Errors in resource combination are frequently made in modern capitalist economies because of imperfect knowledge of local market conditions. In a perfectly competitive world, where maximum efficiency is a condition for survival, such blunders will not occur in the long run, but we live in an imperfectly competitive world. In particular, there have been many well-documented cases of multinational corporations building overseas factories with the most modern American technology, a technology which, because of differences in resource availability, is quite unsuited to the overseas situation.

Secondly, the socialist system provides greater potential flexibility of criteria used in the choice of production techniques. Profit maximisation motivates the individual firm in a capitalist society to choose the cheapest resource combination to produce a given output, given the resource prices prevailing in the market. Now it is unusual in capitalist economies for all resources to be priced—some, like the atmosphere, are free. The outcome is that cheap resources, like air and water, are heavily used by industrialists, with resulting environmental pollution. Thus, pollution is a systematic outcome in a capitalist system where no price is put on natural resources like clean air. Of course, socialist countries have pollution problems too, but the planning system provides a potentially powerful means for their solution. An implicit price can be put on pollutive activities, such that the chosen technology differs from those used in capitalist countries; the difference indicating not so much differences in efficiency but differences in social goals. (A variant of this policy may also be applied in capitalist economies, by using taxes to internalise within the market mechanism the polluting effects of different economic activities. However, experience to date has shown how difficult this is in the face of the vested interests of business groups whose profits would suffer from such a policy.)

A similar point relates to non-economic goals embodied in the choice of production technique. Socialists have defended the use of large-scale capital-intensive technology in the Soviet Union as specific policy of national aggrandisement, whereas development of the 'back-yard steel-production' in China was part of a conscious policy for community development and independence. It may therefore be improper to criticise these production policies on narrow grounds of economic efficiency. Indeed, it is sometimes said that one of the great merits of socialist economies is that production decisions may be used to achieve objectives other than purely technical ones associated with the production of particular outputs at minimum cost. Similarly, it is important to examine the equity implications of different systems of economic organisation. Since the distribution of income is normally very uneven in capitalist societies, we must consider whether this violation of equity standards is a price worth paying for possible increases in economic efficiency.

Overall, the case for reliance on the price system as a means of ensuring productive efficiency does not seem particularly weighty. However, it still retains a certain appeal. Even in many parts of the socialist world, prices play a role in the determination of productive techniques. A socialist community in which production decisions are largely decentralised to industrial managers requires prices to be attached to resources, though those prices are set administratively rather than determined by the market mechanism. Yugoslavia is the most commonly cited socialist-based nation where prices play such a major role, but some developments elsewhere in Eastern Europe and the Soviet Union are consistent with this general approach. On the other hand, it has been observed that in the major capitalist countries, market prices are playing a decreasingly important role. The necessity of planning in an economy dominated by large corporations has led to an increased emphasis on 'administered prices', commodity prices determined as part of a promotional package which remain unchanged for long periods despite changes in cost and demand conditions. The result, it is sometimes said, is that resources are allocated through the market but not by it.[9]

These developments have been lumped together into what is sometimes called *'the convergence thesis'*, whereby in terms of their organisational forms the economies of the socialist world (or at least the Soviet and East European sector of it) and the capitalist world are thought to be coming together. There is not general agreement on this point. Probably the most balanced view is to give credence to the convergence thesis as far as the organisational forms of the societies are concerned, but to deny that it results in similar allocation of resources. The important point is that prices under socialism are not derived in the same way as prices under capitalism. Rather, as we saw before, they may embody particular social objectives, as in the case where the price is set very high to discourage the use of a particular input, the use of which has adverse social consequences, or very low to encourage the use of another, the use of which is thought to be conducive to particular social objectives. Thus, prices under socialism may play different roles with respect to resource allocation. As Dobb says, it is 'the question of what is a correct system of pricing of produced inputs . . . (which is of) central importance as a basis for efficient decision, whether decision is centralised or decentralised'.[10]

[9] See, for example, J. K. Galbraith, *The New Industrial State*, Harmondsworth, Penguin Books, 1969, Chapters 16, 17.
[10] M. Dobb, *Welfare Economics and the Economics of Socialism*, Cambs., Cambridge University Press, 1969, p. 251.

CHAPTER FOUR

What?

This chapter deals with how economic systems resolve the question of what should be produced. Given limited resources, a choice must be made between alternative patterns of production. The way in which this should be done has long been a contentious issue. Galbraith, for example, argues that modern capitalism exhibits 'an implacable tendency to provide an opulent supply of some things and a niggardly yield of others. This disparity carries to the point where it is a cause of social discomfort and social unhealth.'[1] This manifests itself most clearly in the imbalance between the supply of private goods such as cars and other consumer durables and the supply of public goods such as education, parks and public transport. Galbraith further contends that 'this disparity between our flow of private and public goods and services is no matter of subjective judgement'.[2] However, this last view is not widely shared. More typically, economists argue that the question of what is an efficient allocation of resources rests upon a value-judgement as to what the optimum composition of output ought to be; therefore, there is no scientific way of proving (or of disproving) that social imbalance exists. Where does the truth lie in matters such as this?

In investigating this question it is useful to distinguish between three separate issues:

(1) identifying the various combinations of goods and services which could be produced with the available resources;

(2) identifying which of these combinations is ideal in some explicitly normative sense;

(3) identifying the principles which determine the commodity combination in particular economic systems, and any causes of divergence between actual and ideal outcomes.

Only when we have investigated these issues are we in a position to comment on the extent to which the composition of society's output is responsive to

[1] J. K. Galbraith, *The Affluent Society*, Harmondsworth, Penguin Books, 1962, p. 206.
[2] ibid.

the needs of the community. The procedure adopted in this chapter is to examine what orthodox economics has to say on each issue. Although economic theory is sometimes held to show that a capitalist economy is responsive to community needs, we will see that economic theory does not actually support this proposition: indeed, to the extent that it is possible to generalise at all about desirable commodity combinations, there would appear to be a strong organisation in favour of *not* allowing the price mechanism to act as the sole arbiter of what is produced. Let us trace the argument through.

Feasible Commodity Combinations

We can deal with the first step quite quickly. The production possibility frontier was introduced in *Figure 1.1* and its relationship with the dimensions of the Edgeworth box depicted in *Figure 2.2*. This curve shows the maximum commodity combinations available from given resources, for the two-commodity case. It is often said to indicate the 'menu of choices' (though this phrase gives a quite misleading impression of the ease with which the community can dictate changes in the production mix). Any commodity combination out-side the frontier is not attainable with the current resources and the current state of technical knowledge. Any combination within the frontier is attainable, but will lead to unemployment, as more of one commodity could be produced without any cut-back in the output of the other. It is the combinations on the frontier which are of most interest: all are technically efficient in that they all leave no resources unemployed.

The slope of the production possibility frontier has important economic significance. It reflects the cost of producing an extra unit of one commodity in terms of the amount of the other commodity foregone. Thus, it provides an indication of the relative costliness of producing additional units of each commodity. The addition to total cost incurred as a result of producing an additional unit of one commodity is known as the *marginal cost*. Therefore, the slope of the production possibility curve (neglecting signs) can be defined as ratio of the marginal costs of producing the two commodities in question. In the case illustrated in *Figure 1.1* it is the marginal cost of bread divided by the marginal cost of wine.

A cautionary note: the production possibility frontier is not so clearly defined as is sometimes implied. It represents the outputs attainable with the society's resources fully employed. But what constitutes full employment? A year contains 8,760 hours, but people working a forty-hour week and taking an annual fortnight's leave would spend only about 2,000 hours at work. Are such people partially unemployed? Clearly, the answer is 'yes' in the sense that more hours could be spent at work, but 'no' in the sense that most people would choose not to spend more time at work. Thus, the availability of labour resources in the economy is not a uniquely measurable variable: it depends on the individual income/leisure choice and that choice itself depends on a number of factors.

Consider for example, the effect of an increase in income tax: this may lead either to an increased or a reduced supply of effort. These two possibilities are depicted graphically in *Figure 4.1* in terms of the conventional indifference curve analysis. The axes measure income and leisure. Positive preferences for both these are displayed, so the indifference curves are of the 'normal' convex to the origin form. The initial equilibrium is shown by the

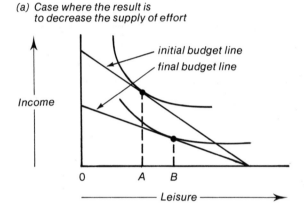

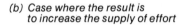

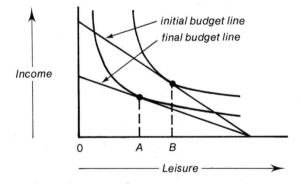

Figure 4.1   The effect on the income-leisure choice of an increase in the rate of income tax

point of tangency between the initial budget line and the highest indifference curve. The effect of the income tax increase is to shift the budget line inwards as shown, because now the same expenditure of effort brings home a smaller 'take-home' pay. The resulting equilibrium may involve more or less leisure than before. In case (a) the consumption of leisure rises (from OA to OB), because the person substitutes leisure which is now relatively 'cheap', for work which is now relatively expensive in terms of the effort needed to earn a given income. In case (b) the consumption of leisure falls (from OB to OA), as the person works more in order to maintain a similar income. Some people will fall in each category, while others will make no change to their overall work/leisure allocation. The net effect is indeterminate. We may conclude that an increase in income taxes may change the supply of labour but the direction of the change cannot be determined on the basis of theoretical analysis alone.

This serves to illustrate the 'fuzzy' nature of the production possibility frontier. Its position depends on a number of socio-economic factors, of which the structure of the income-tax system is only one. In these circumstances the production possibility frontier is best regarded as a broad band, as shown in *Figure 4.2* with an outer limit (BD) and an inner limit (AC), both of which may be hard to specify precisely.

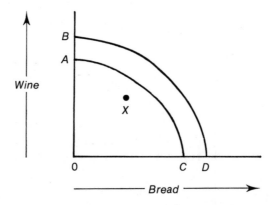

Figure 4.2   The range of full-employment production possibilities

Economic systems vary in relation to what is considered to be the desirable limit of production possibilities. One aspect of this is illustrated by the contrasting attitudes to economic development in capitalist and Maoist ideology. Gurley makes the point as follows: '. . . there is a heavy emphasis in Capitalist development . . . on raising the national output, on producing "things" in ever-increasing amounts. Man is another capital good, an input in the productive engine that grinds out commodities . . . In Maoist eyes, economic development can best be attained by giving prominence to men rather than "things" . . .

Maoists seem perfectly willing to pursue the goal of transforming man even though it is temporarily at the expense of some economic growth.'[3] In terms of conventional microeconomic analysis this would seem to imply that capitalist systems can be expected to define full employment in terms of the outer limits of the production possibility 'band'; *BD* in *Figure 4.2*. (Of course, it does not follow that they will always *achieve* some commodity combination on this frontier. On the contrary, the recurrent tendency to unemployment suggests that outcomes such as point *X* in *Figure 4.2* will be common.)

Optimal Commodity Combinations

Which of the feasible commodity combinations is best for the community? To determine this requires an explicit statement of the criterion by which we can say that one set of commodities is better than another. The most usual criterion is that of consumer preferences, *i.e.*, the best commodity combination is that which is in closest accord with the pattern of consumers' preferences. This is very reasonable in principle; the problems are associated with the identification of preferences for a commodity consisting of many consumers with varied tastes.

But let us begin with the simplest possible situation; a one-person two-commodity community. (We are back on Man Friday's island and Crusoe has not yet arrived. Happy days!) For simplicity, we make the conventional assumption that the production possibility frontier can be represented as a single line. Friday's indifference curves showing his preferences for the two commodities, bread and wine, can be superimposed on this frontier, as shown in *Figure 4.3*.

The ideal is obviously to produce and consume *OA* bread and *OB* wine, this being the commodity combination corresponding to the point of tangency between the production possibility frontier and the highest attainable indifference curve. At this point, the rate at which bread and wine can be substituted in production exactly equals the rate at which the consumer would be prepared to substitute them in consumption. This means that the best combinations of commodities is being produced when the relative production costs of the last unit of each are equal to the relative utility associated with the last unit of each. Thus, we can indicate the optimum condition as follows:

$$\frac{\text{marginal utility of bread}}{\text{marginal utility of wine}} = \frac{\text{marginal cost of bread}}{\text{marginal cost of wine}}$$

According to orthodox economic theory, this indicates the overall optimum

[3] J. Gurley, Capitalist and Maoist Economic Development, *Monthly Review*, February 1971, pp. 15-35.

with respect to efficiency in product selection. Fulfilment of these conditions, it is argued, secures an optimal resource allocation.

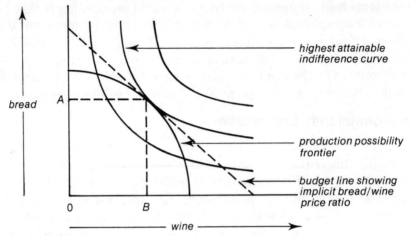

Figure 4.3   Welfare analysis of one-person community

We have been studying a very simple case. The next step is to raise the question whether a similar criterion is operable in a multiple-person community. This issue is often dodged. The indifference curves are relabelled *'community indifference curves'*, the left hand side of the above equality condition is reinterpreted as the rate at which 'the community' is prepared to substitute commodities, and academic tranquility rules again. But not so fast! What is this thing called the community, and how are 'its' preferences and the rate at which 'it' will substitute commodities identified?

We can distinguish three main ways in which attempts have been made to establish an explicit link between individual and community preferences.

Method 1   Identifying community preferences by aggregation of the preferences of individuals who comprise that community.

This involves the identification of the preference orderings of all individuals for all relevant commodity combinations, and the aggregation of such information into a statement on the determinants of collective welfare. Obviously this procedure poses tremendous problems, since individuals are often unable or unwilling to provide the required information. However, there is a more fundamental problem. The procedure itself is conceptually unsound because ordinal utilities are not amenable to aggregation. If we cannot measure preferences on a cardinal scale—and orthodox economists agree that we cannot—then any form of aggregation of preferences is ruled out. This is a general problem with ordinal measurement. If your position in a school class is first in economics, fourth in mathematics and fourteenth in English, are you a better student than someone placed second, fifth and sixth in corresponding subjects? We cannot say with the same generality that would be possible if we knew the cardinal scores in each subject.

Method 2 Identifying community preferences by observation of market behaviour.

This procedure involves the derivation of a collective preference ordering from study of market behaviour. If, when apples and pears both have the same price, more apples than pears are sold, we may conclude that the community as a whole prefers apples. Similarly, when the price of apples rises relative to pears we can observe the rate at which consumers substitute pears for apples and deduce from this something more about the nature of community preferences. Or can we?

One problem with this procedure is that the result is bounded by the choices currently available to the community. Community preferences for commodities not currently marketed cannot be recorded. This is sometimes said to give the approach a conservative bias and, indeed, the function of legitimising the existing pattern of commodity production, whatever that might be.

Of even greater importance is the bias introduced by this method because of its failure to abstract from the existing distribution of income. Income provides the means through which consumers in a market system are able to express their preferences. What this means is that in all circumstances, except the unlikely one where all consumers' tastes are identical, the revealed pattern of community preferences will be different for every distribution of income. To take a very simple example of a two-person community, assume I like apples and you like pears. If I am wealthy and you are poor, the community will show an apparent preference for apples, whereas the opposite result will occur if you are the more wealthy. Adding consumers' preferences according to the weighting system offered by the existing income distribution is shown to generate information on only one possible community preference pattern.

Moreover, to aggregate revealed preferences given the existing distribution of income is to put an implicit seal of approval on the existing situation. This is not acceptable, because what we are seeking is to identify what is the socially optimum pattern of production and consumption: in effect, we would be assuming what we are seeking to examine. Mishan generalises this point as follows: 'there is a bias in favour of the status quo whenever one aims to bring the economy closer to the optimum using the existing set of prices since this set of prices itself emerges from the income distribution'.[4] Such a bias is only acceptable to the apoligist.

[4] E. J. Mishan, *The Costs of Economics Growth*, Harmondsworth, Penguin Books, 1969, p. 78.

Method 3   Identifying community preferences through the political process.

The difficulties involved in aggregating individual preferences and in deriving information about community preferences from market behaviour have led some economists to write of welfare economics as a dead-end branch of the discipline. Others have sought to widen the discipline and, in particular, to break down the barriers between economics and politics which they regard as inhibiting progress in understanding community objectives. This is highly commendable. However, it must be admitted that the application of economics to the analysis of political behaviour has been rather unproductive to date, despite (or perhaps because of) the studies by Downs, Buchanan and Tullock and others.[5]

As has often been noted, there are important practical problems with existing political machinery as a means of identifying consumer preferences. These include:

(1) the infrequency of elections;
(2) the difficulty of isolating attitudes to particular issues in elections characterised by policy 'packages';
(3) 'gerrymandering' in the delineation of electorates.[6]

There are also some problems of a fundamental conceptual nature which are relevant in this respect. The theoretical association between individual and social choice in democratic systems is fraught with difficulty. The most important contribution from an economist on this issue is usually held to be that of Kenneth Arrow.[7] Arrow's book is a complex piece of work but its main conclusions are intuitively not too difficult to understand. One strand relates to the problem of *transitivity* in collective choices. Transitivity is the condition that if X is preferred to Y and Y to Z, we can deduce that X is preferred to Z. This assumption underlies all the conventional indifference curve theory of consumers' demand, but it only creates a real problem when we are concerned with collective preference patterns.

Consider the following simple illustration.[8] Three individuals (A, B and C) are confronted with three policies (X, Y and Z). They are asked to express

---

[5] See A. Downs, *An Economic Theory of Democracy*, New York, Harper and Row, 1957, and J. M. Buchanan and G. Tullock, *The Calculus of Consent*, Ann Arbor, Michigan University Press, 1962.

[6] A striking example is provided by the 1972 elections for the State government in Queensland. The systematic bias in the delineation of constituencies led to the result that the Australian Labor Party polled 48 per cent of the total votes cast and got thirty-three seats: the Liberal-Country Party coalition polled 41 per cent and was returned with forty-seven seats.

[7] K. J. Arrow, *Social Choice and Individual Values*, New York, Wiley, 1951.

[8] Adapted from S. G. Sturmey & D. W. Pearce, *Economic Analysis*, London, McGraw-Hill, 1966, Chapter 4.

their preferences between various pairs of the policies, and the outcomes are shown as under:

Individual	Explicit preferences	Implicit preferences
A	$X > Y, Y > Z$	$X > Z$
B	$Y > Z, Z > X$	$Y > X$
C	$Z > X, X > Y$	$Z > Y$

Note that, given two explicit preferences we can deduce the third preference by application of the transitivity rule. Now, if the individuals were asked to vote on the various policies, the outcome would be as under:

Policy	Votes for	Votes against
$X > Y$	2	1
$Y > Z$	2	1
$X > Z$	1	2

Thus, the majority of the community shows a preference for X over Y, and for Y over Z. Application of the transitivity rule would lead us to deduce that X would be preferred to Z, but this is not so: if asked to vote for X or Z, the majority of the community would vote for Z. Thus, if the logic of the transitivity rule is accepted, social choice cannot be derived from individual preferences.

The association between the democratic process and community welfare becomes somewhat confused in these circumstances. The root problem is clearly in the assumption that preferences are only amenable to ordinal measurement. In order to derive a statement of collective preferences from information on individual preferences we need to take account of the *intensity* of preferences of the different individuals and groups within the community in question.[9] Some have suggested that these intensities are reflected in the political process through *pressure group* behaviour: it is argued that individuals with very intense preferences for some particular course of action will normally express this by banding together specifically in order to influence public policy. But the argument is hardly convincing. Some social groups have

---

[9] Realising these sort of difficulties associated with ordinal utility measurement, some economists have sought to revive interest in the analysis based on cardinal measurement. In particular, there is growing recognition that economists must concern themselves with interpersonal comparisons of utility if they are to be of help in the formulation of public policies which benefit some people at the expense of others. See, for example, B. Ward, *What's Wrong With Economics*, London, Macmillan, 1972, and S. K. Nath, *A Perspective on Welfare Economics*, London, Macmillan, 1973.

more cohesion, facilities and expertise in such matters than others. For example, it does not follow that a person's preference for continuing to live in his existing house is not intense because he does not form a pressure group to prevent expressway construction from destroying it. The propensity to engage in such activities tend to reflect social class position as well as intensity of preference.

We are left with the conclusion that any identification of collective preferences through existing political machinery is fraught with difficulty. This is particularly true where social class divisions are important. As Parkin notes, 'in a class-stratified society the very notion of a national interest is highly problematic'.[10] In these circumstances any general theoretical solution to the question 'what is the ideal combination of goods and services?' cannot easily be identified. What are we left with? Broadly, two circumstances where the pattern of community preferences can be readily identified:

(1)   where all individual preference patterns are materially the same;
(2)   where all individuals are prepared to convey to one member of the community the right to determine what is best for the whole community.[11]

The first situation is usually discounted as highly improbable, (though it is not as ridiculous as might at first appear because, as noted in Chapter 2, many apparent differences in consumers' preferences reflect income differences rather than differences in tastes). If the second situation is ruled out by some other criterion (as Arrow and Samuelson argue that it should be because of its totalitarian connotations) we must conclude that community preferences cannot be identified on the basis of individual preferences as they are expressed either in the market or in the 'ballot-box'.

Nevertheless, economists typically continue to adhere to the rule that optimal allocation involves that particular combination of activities such that the ratio of marginal utilities for any pair of commodities equals the ratio of marginal costs involved in producing them. In particular, this rule is retained as the principle rationale for having an economy organised on competitive lines. The next section of this chapter examines this proposition.

---

[10]   F. Parkin, *Class Inequality and Political Order*, London, Paladin Books, 1972, p. 135.

[11]   The ever-ingenious Samuelson adds a third circumstance using the analagy between society and the family as a collection of individuals. 'If within the family there can be assumed to take place an optimal reallocation of income so as to keep each member's dollar expenditure of equal ethical worth then there can be derived for the whole family a set of well-behaved indifference contours relating the totals of what it consumes: the family can be said to *act as if* it maximises such a group preference function. The same argument will apply to all of society if optimum reallocation of income can be assumed to keep equal the ethical worth of persons marginal dollar', P. Samuelson, Social Indifference Curves, *The Quarterly Journal of Economics*, February, 1956, pp. 1-22. Now assume that cows can fly . . . .

Product Selection in a Perfectly Competitive Economy

How does a society determine which of the alternative feasible commodity combinations will actually be produced? In a pure market economy, this is determined by the price system. Each consumer expresses the strength of his preferences for different commodities through the price he is prepared to pay for each. These prices also serve the function of providing incentives to producers to supply various commodities. The outcome is a particular combination of goods reflecting the amounts consumers will offer for different quantities of particular commodities and the amounts required by producers to provide those commodities. This is the situation sometimes approvingly described as 'consumer sovereignty', whereby the pattern of production is seen as responsive to the autonomous needs and tastes of the consumers. As one popular textbook puts it, 'the consumer is, so to speak, the king . . . each is a voter who uses his money as votes to get the things done that he wants done'.[12]

This sounds very soothing. But let us look a little more closely at how this process works out in different market situations. We start with the situation of *perfect competition*. This is a theoretical market structure which has played an extremely important role in the development of orthodox economic theory. It is defined by the following conditions:

(1) so many buyers and sellers of the product that no one of them is large enough relative to the total market to influence the price;

(2) all units of the product are identical;

(3) no constraints on buyers and sellers entering or leaving the market;

(4) no other non-market restraints on demand, supply and product price.

In this situation the price of each commodity is determined by aggregate demand and supply in the market and no individual producer has sufficient power to influence it. Producers can only decide how much they will sell at the given price. This is actually quite a simple decision in principle. If we assume that they seek to maximise profits (which is a very reasonable assumption, since producers are unlikely to last long in such a competitive situation if they do not), the output selected will be that where the marginal cost of production equals price (given that the marginal cost is rising as output increases). This is illustrated in *Figure 4.4*.

Beyond a certain level of output the marginal cost (defined earlier as the addition to total cost incurred as a result of producing an additional unit of output) can be expected to rise as output increases. This reflects the general

---

[12] P. Samuelson, *Economics: An Introductory Analysis*, 6th Edition, New York, McGraw-Hill, 1964, p. 56.

rule that, as more and more units of a variable input (say labour) are added to an input which is temporarily fixed for the individual producer (say, capital or land), the costs of producing additional units of output will eventually rise.

The producer could stop at output level *OA* in *Figure 4.4* but he would be making a profit on the last unit of output produced, since the price he obtains for it is above the cost of producing it. It would be in his interest to expand output. However, if he were to produce output *OC* he would be making a loss on the last unit of output (and some of the previous units), since at that output marginal cost exceeds price. The profit-maximising output is *OB*, where marginal cost equals price: total profits are diminished by any deviation from that level.

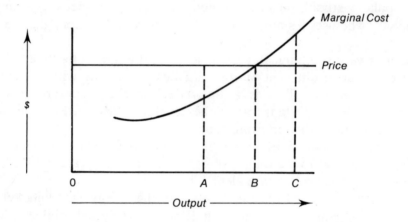

Figure 4.4   The individual producer in a perfectly competitive market

We return now to the normative question of optimal allocation. Does this perfectly competitive situation conform to the rule for optimal allocation established earlier in this chapter? Yes. If there are two industries (bread and wine production) and firms in both produce up to the point where marginal cost equals price, then:

$$\frac{\text{marginal cost of bread}}{\text{marginal cost of wine}} = \frac{\text{price of bread}}{\text{price of wine}}$$

If consumers act in the 'ideal' manner described in Chapter 2, they allocate their expenditure so that:

$$\frac{\text{price of bread}}{\text{price of wine}} = \frac{\text{marginal utility of bread}}{\text{marginal utility of wine}}$$

Putting these two equations together we find:

$$\frac{\text{marginal utility of bread}}{\text{marginal utility of wine}} = \frac{\text{marginal cost of bread}}{\text{marginal cost of wine}}$$

This is the condition for optimal allocation. It can be generalised from the two-commodity case to the multiple-commodity case with little difficulty. Hence, the standard conclusion of Paretian economics; that perfectly competitive markets are conducive to the production of the ideal commodity combination.

However, as every student of economics with a healthy scepticism notes, the perfectly competitive situation is very rare. The remainder of this chapter is concerned with the introduction of a little more realism. We proceed in three stages:

(1)   consideration of the effects of imperfect competition among producers;
(2)   consideration of the effects of advertising and other activities of producers designed to increase consumer demands;
(3)   consideration of the problems raised by the existence of so-called 'external effects'.

The Effect of Imperfect Competition

Perfectly competitive markets are inherently unstable. Any self-interested producer will naturally seek to engage in extra-market activities to reduce the severity of the constraints on his or her behaviour. Thus, collusive activities arise: producers may make agreements with each other to maintain prices above the competitive level, they may collude to lobby the government for subsidies to the industry, they may seek to make direct agreements with suppliers or consumers which give them a competitive advantage, or they may seek to take over other competitors so as to attain market power.

The result is that *oligopoly* (an industry dominated by a few large firms) and *monopoly* (an industry in which there is only one firm) are the more characteristic market structures. Are such industries conducive to optimal product selection in the same way as perfect competition? Orthodox economists have tackled this question as follows (for brevity the analysis is limited to the monopoly case, though the conclusions are generally also held to be applicable to oligopolistic markets).

The equilibrium for the profit maximising monopolist is not where price equals marginal cost, but where *marginal revenue* equals marginal cost, marginal revenue being defined as the addition to total revenue incurred as a result of selling one additional unit of output. The marginal revenue will normally be less than the price, because it is assumed that the monopolist must reduce price in order to expand sales and this price reduction is assumed to apply not only to the marginal unit of output but to all units of output. (Unless resale of the commodity is impossible this last assumption is quite reasonable because the monopolist is prevented from discriminating between consumers by the possibility of some of them buying at the lowest price and re-selling to other consumers.) A simple illustration is as follows. The producer of a particular commodity markets it at $1 per unit and sells ten units, giving him a total revenue of $10. In order to sell one more unit he must cut the price to 95c per unit. Then he sells eleven units at 95c giving him a total revenue of $10.45. The marginal revenue is the increase or total revenue divided by the increase in the number of items sold *i.e.*, 45c. The normal relationship between price and marginal revenue is illustrated in *Figure 4.5*. The output where profits are maximised is shown as *OA*, marginal cost being equal to marginal revenue at this level.

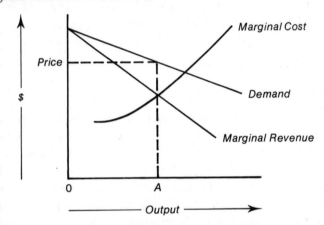

Figure 4.5   Equilibrium of a monopoly producer

If some industries are competitively organised and others are characterised by monopoly, there will be a misallocation of resources. Consider two industries; bread production which is monopolistic, and wine which is perfectly competitive. The equilibrium output in the first case is that at which marginal cost equals marginal revenue and the equilibrium output in the latter case is that at which marginal cost equals price. Putting them together, we find:

$$\frac{\text{marginal cost of bread}}{\text{marginal cost of wine}} > \frac{\text{price of bread}}{\text{price of wine}}$$

The equality necessary for optimal resource allocation does not hold. Too many of the community's resources are used in wine production relative to production. This occurs because the monopolist restricts production ᴊer to increase price above the perfectly competitive level.

ᴊ all industries are equally monopolistic, this sort of resource misallocaᴊn will not occur. If the ratio of marginal revenue to price is the same in each industry, the equilibrium will occur where the ratio of marginal costs between industries equals the ratio of prices. Say, for example, price is 50 per cent above marginal revenue in each industry, then the profit maximising output is determined where:

$$\text{marginal cost} = \text{marginal revenue} = 0.67 \text{ price}.$$

If this holds true in both the bread and wine industries, then:

$$\frac{\text{marginal cost of bread}}{\text{marginal cost of wine}} = \frac{\text{marginal revenue of bread}}{\text{marginal revenue of wine}} = \frac{\text{price of bread}}{\text{price of wine}}$$

This is consistent with the criterion for optimal resource allocation. However, it should be noted that such a situation may cause problems elsewhere in the economy. For example, it is likely to lead to unemployment in labour markets, because all producers are restricting output below perfectly competitive levels. Also it is likely to intensify problems of income inequality in the society, since consumers face higher prices than in the competitive situation and producers reap higher profits.

So much for the orthodox analysis of the allocative effect of imperfect competition. It is certainly neat but there is a strong element of unrealism. As Galbraith notes in his most recent book, the most common grievances about monopolists and oligopolists are not that they restrict output, but rather that their actions lead to undesirably *high* levels of production from the viewpoint of community welfare.[13] The resolution of this apparent paradox lies in an analysis of advertising and other sales promotion activities. For any given level of consumers' demand for their products, monopolists and oligopolists can be expected to restrict output and raise prices above competitive levels, but the level of consumers' demand will not normally be the same. On the contrary, monopolists and oligopolists can be expected to engage in activities specifically designed to stimulate the demand for their products.

Sales Promotion Activities

It is unreasonable to assume, as most of the orthodox analysis does, that producers will take the demand for their products as given. A profit-maximising firm will seek to increase the demand for his product through *advertising* and other sales promotion activities.

[13] J. K. Galbraith, *Economics and the Public Purpose*, New York, Houghton Mifflin, 1973, p. 119.

The central issue in an economic evaluation of sales promotion activities is often said to be the distinction between informative and persuasive advertising; conventionally the former is seen as leading to a more efficient allocation of resources while the latter is seen as leading to inefficiency. The distinction is both conceptually and empirically difficult to draw. As Needham argues: 'Preferences are necessarily formed on the basis of information: whether such information is informative or persuasive is a matter of semantics'.[14] However, to regard this as the central issue is to throw a smoke-screen over the more important distinction: between biased and unbiased advertising. Taking this viewpoint, all commercial advertising can be expected to be in the former category. (This is not in itself a criticism of advertisers but simply a recognition that commercial advertising, being profit-oriented, can be expected to lay stress on those aspects of a product which will lead to high sales and to ignore those which are likely to deter potential consumers.)

Economists differ in their assessment of the impact of biased advertising on consumer welfare. A fairly widely held view is typified in the following statement: 'The consumer has no quarrel with advertising as such. His basic quarrel is simply that this medium has been misused. As a whole, it has not been designed to inform, but has been powered for a lesser objective—the promotion of brands. And, being so powered, it has less often led to consumer enlightenment than to consumer bewilderment.'[15]

However, more radical commentators argue that advertising fulfils a necessary function in helping to absorb part of the surplus production of the capitalist system. It is necessary in order to maintain the high consumption levels on which the system depends. As such any criticism of commercial advertising and its effects is by extension a criticism of capitalist organisation. In the words of Baran and Sweezy: 'Advertising in all of its aspects cannot be meaningfully dealt with as some undesirable excrescence of the economic system which could be removed if "we" would only make up our minds to get rid of it. The very offspring of monopoly capitalism, the inevitable by-product of the decline of price competition, advertising constitutes as much an integral part of the system as the giant corporation itself.'[16]

Funnily enough, an almost identical view is sometimes heard from the defenders of commercial advertising: 'Advertising is merely a means to an end, and the end is a consumption-oriented people. Thus, the question of whether

---

[14] D. Needham, *Economic Analysis and Industrial Structure*, New York, Holt, Rinehart & Winston, 1969, p. 161.

[15] C. E. Warne, Advertising—A Critic's View, Journal of Marketing, Vol. 26, October 1962, reprinted in R. S. Iman & R. E. Murphy (Eds.), *The Economic Process: Inquiry and Challenge*, Glenview, Illinois, Scott, Foresman & Company, 1969, pp. 40-43.

[16] P. Baran and P. Sweezy, *Monopoly Capital*, Harmondsworth, Penguin Books, p. 126.

or not advertising contradicts our value-system hinges on the legitimacy of high-level consumption as a social goal . . . The critics of advertising are not really criticising advertising: they are criticising the American value-system itself.'[17] So be it!

The analysis of advertising and its consequences for resource allocation has been taken up most enthusiastically by Galbraith. He argues that it has shifted the power to determine the composition of output from consumers to producers. Instead of the producers responding to the revealed preferences of consumers, the consumers become the responsive parties. 'The individual's wants, though superficially they may seem to originate with him, are ultimately at the behest of the mechanism that supplies them. In the most specific manifestation the producing firm controls its own prices in the market and goes beyond to persuade the consumer to the appropriate responding behaviour. But it also selects and designs products with a view to what can be so priced and made subject to persuasion. And it does this in a society in which the strongly iterated and reiterated praise of goods makes them seem important for happiness, and thus makes the individual attentive to claims in this regard.'[18] Taking up the theme, Mishan argues that 'to continue to regard the market, in an affluent and growing economy, as primarily a want-satisfying mechanism is to close one's eyes to the more important fact that it has become a want-creating mechanism'.[19]

To the extent that persuasive advertising has led to the replacement of 'consumers' sovereignty' by 'producers' sovereignty' in major sectors of the economy, faith in the market as an allocative device must necessarily be undermined. Certainly 'the revised sequence' (consumption being adjusted to production rather than production to consumption), is very uncomfortable for the orthodox economic theory which is normally invoked in defence of the market economy. The Paretian assumption that all individuals are the best judge of their own welfare becomes an increasingly dubious starting point. More importantly, the assumption that consumers' preferences are formulated independently of the economic system becomes totally untenable. To quote Mishan again: 'These new wants (generated by advertising) may be deemed imaginary or they may be alleged to be as real as the original set of wants. What cannot be gain-said, however, is that the foundation necessary to enable economists to infer and measure increases in individual or social welfare crumbles up in these circumstances. Only as given wants remain constant

---

[17] T. A. Petit and A. Zakon, Advertising and Social Values, *Journal of Marketing*, Vol. 26, October 1962, also reprinted in R. S. Iman & R. E. Murphy (Eds.), *The Economic Process, Inquiry and Challenge*, Glenview, Illinois, Scott, Foresman & Company, 1969, pp. 37-40.

[18] J. K. Galbraith, Economics as a System of Belief, *The American Economic Review: Papers and Proceedings*, May 1970, pp. 469-478.

[19] E. J. Mishan, *The Costs of Economic Growth*, Harmondsworth, Penguin Books, 1969, p. 149.

and productive activity serves to narrow the margin of discontent between appetites and their gratifications are we justified in talking of an increase in welfare. And one may reasonably conjecture that unremitting efforts directed towards stimulating aspirations and enlarging appetites may cause them to grow faster than the possibilities for their gratification, so increasing over time the margin of social discontent.'[20]

External Effects

In Chapter 2 we saw that interdependence of consumers' preferences under-mines the distributional efficiency of the price system. In Chapter 3 we saw that spillovers of one production activity on to the costs of other producers cause inefficiency in the selection of production techniques. Here we see that these same sorts of interdependence reduce the possibility of the ideal combina-tion of goods and services being produced.

It must be stressed that the problem of 'external effects' is a problem of an *imperfect* market economy. If all activities having beneficial consequences for consumers' welfare bore a price which reflected what those consumers were prepared to pay to maintain that activity, there would be no allocative inefficiency associated with external economies. Similarly if all persons con-ducting activities having adverse effects on consumers' welfare had to pay the consumers a price which fully compensated them for their loss of welfare, there would be no problem of external diseconomies. But this is not the case in practice. External effects are a recurrent problem. Because the market does not internalise all 'spillovers' there are systematic tendencies towards resource misallocation. Too many resources will be directed to the production and con-sumption of goods and services with adverse 'spillover' effects (for example, motor cars) and too few to the production and consumption of goods and ser-vices with beneficial 'spillover' effects (for example, education).

One outcome of reliance on a price system which fails to internalise these spillovers is a deteriorating environmental quality. Clean air and water are free goods: it is not surprising that they are used up in such quantities. The users do not normally have to compensate society for the adverse spillovers. Yes, the price system is often a fairly flexible allocative mechanism, but it allocates resources to ends which are not in the best interests of the community as a whole.

Mention must also be made of a rather special type of resource misallocation associated with the problem of external effects. This relates to what are normally known as *'public goods'*. Such goods must be collectively consumed,

[20] E. J. Mishan, *The Costs of Economic Growth*, Harmondsworth, Penguin Books, 1969, p. 150.

and a price cannot be charged because individuals cannot be barred from using them. As such they will not be provided at all in a pure market economy. Even Adam Smith, generally regarded as the high-priest of *laissez-faire* economics, recognised that the State has 'the duty of maintaining and erecting certain public institutions which it can never be for the interest of any individual or small number of individuals to erect and maintain, because the profit could never repay the expense to any individual or small number of individuals; though it may frequently do much more than repay it to a great society'.[21] There is debate about the appropriate range of such activities, from museums, parks, street-cleaning, fire and police services to 'defence', health, education, and so on. Whatever the scope of these public goods, they clearly constitute another source of market failure.

Some Implications for Policy

These last remarks bring us back to the issue of 'social balance' with which this chapter began. In going through the full circle what have we learned? We have learned that orthodox economic theory is fraught with difficulties when applied to the analysis of collective choice, but that, to the extent that general conclusions are possible, systematic tendencies to inefficiency in product selection are to be expected in a capitalist economy. The main sources of market distortion and market failure are associated with imperfect competition, advertising, external effects and the provision of public goods. These go a long way towards explaining the cause of the imbalance between 'private wealth and public squalor'. The supply of consumer durables is typically in the hands of large corporations who seek to stimulate demand for their products through extensive sales promotion activities. In the production and consumption of these goods, external diseconomies arise, leading to degradation of the physical and social environment. By contrast, the supply of goods giving rise to external economies is niggardly because the system over-prices them. Public goods are especially poorly provided since, even when governments do take responsibility for them (and they often do not), they are not usually advertised in the seductive way that characterises the products of the private corporate sector. The overall result is a systematic tendency towards resource misallocation.

Since the price mechanism cannot guarantee the right combination of goods and services, product selection must necessarily become an explicitly *political* question. There are various ways in which this argument can be taken up. Perhaps the mildest proposition is that it indicates a need for a more extended

---

[21] A. Smith, *An Inquiry into the True Nature and Causes of the Wealth of Nations*, Edited by E. Cannan, New York, Random House, 1937, p. 651.

debate than now exists on the proper allocation of public funds, whatever the size of the public sector. The normal practice in most countries is for the allocation between government departments (education, health, 'defence', and so on) to be based on last year's allocation: each department tenders an estimate based on past experience plus some mark-up, and the Treasury makes downwards adjustments to each estimate when preparing the overall budget. However, because resource allocation is such a crucial question, it can be argued that it should be brought into more open debate. This suggestion does not solve the problem of how collective choices are to be made. However, it does put useful emphasis on the need to recognise that allocation of public funds is not a purely technical decision, but rather one which involves a trade-off between social objectives.

A social democrat would go further and argue that a strong case has been provided for an extension of the role of the public sector. Thus, it has been revealed that the price system not only fails to meet the criterion of efficient product selection (except by the most amazing chance); it tends *systematically* to misallocate resources. This can then be used as an argument for an extension of public control through such policies as the nationalisation of industry. Such a policy is clearly no panacea of itself but does open the opportunity for decisions about the quantity of output of each industry to be determined in relation to community objectives rather than purely in relation to private profits. Again, the difficulty of identifying collective objectives remains, but this solution has appeal to those who see planning by bodies accountable to the electorate as the best means of bringing under public decision the broad allocation of national output.

Radicals take a rather different tack. Papandreau's view is typical: 'The State in paternalistic capitalism has become a cog in the process of private planning by the corporate establishment. Its domestic tasks call for the socialisation of the research and development costs of private enterprise, the provision of an increasingly elaborate infrastructure, the control of aggregate demand, and the effectuation of industrial peace (that is the development of a mechanism for settling industrial disputes without disruption of the economic process).'[22] Add to this its role in 'defence' and one gets a view of an increasingly interlinked relationship between business and government, typified by what has been called the 'military-industrial complex'. In circumstances where you cannot say where business ends and government begins, it may seem rather naïve to call for an extension of the public sector. Rather, radicals argue that it is more realistic to take the view that modern capitalism is a

---

[22] A. G. Papandreau, *Paternalistic Capitalism*, Minneapolis, University of Minnesota Press, 1972, p. 91.

jointly-managed economy and, to the extent that it is irrational and exploitive, that the private and public sectors are equally responsible. The solution is seen in revolution rather than reform.

Of course, socialist systems have their own problems regarding the efficiency of product selection. Indeed, the choice of commodity combinations is bound to be a particularly difficult one under socialism because of the greater emphasis on administrative decision rather than markets. The absence of a sensitive mechanism through which consumers can express their preferences can be a real problem. However, the problem of inefficiency is likely to be most concentrated in those areas where it matters least. The demand for necessities or for broad types of goods is generally fairly constant and fairly easily calculated, so that the appropriate supply in these cases can be rather easily determined. On the other hand, the demand for luxuries and for particular varieties of goods within these broad categories is volatile and difficult to calculate. It is in these latter respects that administrators are likely to make bad decisions regarding supply. But it is in these latter respects that bad decisions matter least, since consumers' welfare is less vulnerable to misallocation in the detailed composition of output than it is to misallocation of basic necessities and broad types of goods. As Dobb says 'where adjustment of supply to preferences is important, it is also relatively easy; where it is difficult it would seem to be of a relatively minor order of importance'.[23]

Socialist economies are also said to lead to a reduced range of choice, because diversity is not the natural outcome that it is under capitalism. Again, there is considerable truth in this. However, caution is needed. It is important to question how wide is the range of *effective* choice under capitalist systems. Commercial advertising creates particular problems in this respect. Lipton suggests that individual choice requires that the person 'has weighted the consequences of two or more of a set of possible actions (and) has reached and can execute a decision based on preferences among the consequences assessed'.[24] By this standard many consumers' actions do not constitute choices at all: rather they are programmed, thoughtless or random responses.

Moreover, many of the so-called 'choices' which consumers face in capitalist systems are in many respects quite trivial. There is a natural tendency for convergence in product design: marketing executives know that a new product must be basically similar to previous products, but with small changes in styling, packaging, etc. Lipsey suggests that, particularly in oligopolistic markets, this tendency towards convergent behaviour is sufficiently general to warrant a name(!): 'the principle of minimum differentiation'. His own

[23] M. Dobb, *Political Economy and Capitalism*, London, Routledge, 1937, p. 314.
[24] M. Lipton, *Assessing Economic Performance*, London, Staples Press, 1968, p. 107.

prime example is that of British radio which (at the time of writing) was a three-station monopoly under the control of a public corporation, and British television which was based on competition between two stations in any one area. 'It was found that the three stations of the monopolised radio produced very little similarity between the products offered at any one time, while the two stations of British television produced almost identical products for a great deal of the time. Thus, at a randomly selected time of the day the radio listener was likely to have two or three varied possibilities open to him, while the television viewer was likely to be forced to choose between two almost identical programmes.'[25] *Newsweek* and *Time* magazines provide another excellent example of convergence bordering on duplication. In these circumstances we must be careful not to confuse product differentiation with a wide range of effective choice.

[25] R. G. Lipsey, *An Introduction to Positive Economics*, Third Edition, London, Weidenfeld and Nicolson, 1971, p. 308.

CHAPTER FIVE

Where?

The spatial dimension of resource allocation has been accorded much less attention by economic theorists than the dimensions considered in the preceding three chapters. However, the importance of the location of economic activities is being increasingly acknowledged. Technological improvements in transport and communications constantly widen the choices of individuals making location decisions, while these same improvements in communications make us increasingly conscious of the inequalities of material standards in different parts of the world. Thus, the question of 'where' has important social implications as well as being of imminent concern to each individual or organisation contemplating the creation or relocation of any economic activity. A rational businessman operating in a capitalist system will appraise the advantages and disadvantages of alternative sites and select that which matches his preferences most closely (whether those preferences be for maximum profits, maximum sales, proximity of workplace to a golf course, or whatever). Similarly, individual household location decisions may involve the consideration of both economic and non-economic considerations. The outcome of these self-interested location decisions is a distribution of population and employment which may give rise to economic and social problems for the community as a whole. There may, for example, be interregional inequality in incomes, localised unemployment, urban congestion and undesirable quantities of pollution. What is an efficient allocation of resources in space for each individual, may not lead to an efficient spatial allocation for the community as a whole. This raises the question of whether reliance on the price mechanism is the best means of answering this question of where economic activities should be located.

Economic theory has often been used to provide support for locational *laissez-faire*. A typical statement is that of Henderson and Ledebur: 'the microeconomic function of allocation of economic activities through space is performed better through the pricing mechanism than through centralised planning or allocative policy'.[1] Greenhut takes an even stronger stance: he

---

[1] W. L. Henderson and L. C. Ledebur, *Urban Economics: Processes and Problems*, New York, John Wiley, 1972, p. 199.

concludes a long book on location analysis by saying that with respect to locational matters, 'a free enterprise system . . . is effective, efficient want-satisfying and perfectly viable'.[2] In an appendix to the same book Greenhut further contends that 'the free enterprise economic system will move inexorably towards optimal results if the proper cultural base, including interpersonal relations . . . are established for it by its government'.[3] (It seems that the people must adjust to the economy rather than the economy to the people!) This chapter is, in effect, an examination of the sort of arguments which are normally held to support such conclusions.

Location and Efficiency

First of all let us look at the theory of location and the ways in which it may be used in the formulation of generalisations about the effects of private enterprise on the spatial allocation of resources. Location theorists usually pay most attention to the firm. The normal justification for this is that, whereas business location decisions are the major driving force in the regional economy, household location decisions can be best understood in terms of a process of adjustment to the pattern of business location. Now, of course, this is quite reasonable in the sense that household location choice is usually constrained by the need for accessibility to workplaces and to retail and service facilities of various kinds. But on the other hand, business locations are strongly influenced by labour availability and distance-to-market considerations. Perhaps the best view is to regard the two sets of location decisions as interdependent. One simply pays initial attention to business location because, in a capitalist economy, changes in the spatial allocation of resources require changes in the location of business as a necessary condition. Ideally, an iterative approach should be used in studying the various sets of decisions.

The basic assumption underlying economic models of business location is the familiar profit maximisation postulate. Typically, firms are considered as choosing a location on the basis of an evaluation of the estimated costs and revenues associated with alternative sites, the one chosen being that where the excess of estimated revenues over estimated costs is maximised. There are a variety of economic models of firm location, but they are mainly variations on the profit maximisation theme. For example, the earliest location theories such as those of Weber and Von Thünen centred on cost minimisation. The firm (or farm) was seen as seeking that location where a given set of productive

---

[2] M. L. Greenhut, *A Theory of the Firm in Economic Space*, New York, Appleton—Century —Crofts, 1970, p. 373.

[3] M. L. Greenhut, op. cit., p. 379.

activities could be conducted at minimum costs. This is consistent with profit maximisation in the special case where revenues are the same in every location. Similarly, the models of Hotelling, Greenhut and others have emphasised the quest for a maximum revenue location in the situation where sellers compete with each other for a given market. This objective is consistent with profit maximisation on the condition that production costs are the same in all locations. Thus, both the least-cost and the maximum-revenue models can be considered to be special cases of the more general profit maximisation model.[4]

The location of households relative to the centres of business activity is also conventionally treated by economists in terms of a maximisation process. Households are seen as seeking a location which maximises their utility. The main differences between the various theories are attributable to the assumptions about what determines the utility associated with different sites. The most common assumption is that utility depends on *accessibility* (subject to income and possibly housing quality constraints).[5] A simple model can be used to show how this determines the spatial structure of urban areas, the land being allocated through the market according to the value placed on accessibility by various users.

Consider *Figure 5.1*. The problem is how an urban land area is allocated as between alternative uses. For simplicity only four uses are considered, and the relationship between the rent which could be paid in each use and distance from the central business district is taken as linear. Thus, the lines X_1, X_2, X_3 and X_4 indicate the relationship between distance and the maximum rent payable for the four uses. The closer the activity to the centre the higher the rent that could be paid. X_1 may be considered to relate to an activity such as commerce, the profitability of which depends crucially on centrality. X_2 may be manufacturing, X_3 residential activity and X_4 agricultural activity. Now, since competition ensures that each piece of land is rented by the highest bidder, all distances from the centre to point A are occupied by commercial activities, AB is occupied by manufacturing, BC by residential activities and CB by farms. If the system is generalised to a two-dimensional space by rotating OD around O, then we get a concentric zone pattern of land uses.

As many urban analysts have noted, this simple pattern is seldom found in

[4] For further discussion of differences between these various models of business location see H. W. Richardson, *Regional Economics*, London, Weidenfeld and Nicolson, 1969, Chapter 4, or H. O. Nourse, *Regional Economics*, New York, McGraw-Hill, 1968, Chapter 2.
[5] Various types of household location models are considered in H. W. Richardson, *Urban Economics*, Harmondsworth, Penguin Books, 1971, Chapters 1 and 2. See also, W. Alonso, *Location and Land Use: Towards a General Theory of Land Rent*, Cambridge Mass., Harvard University Press, 1964.

practice. Typically, the system is distorted by topographical features and the particular form of the transport network. Also, radial sectors tend to be developed as particular types of land use originating near a city centre migrate within the same sector away from the centre. Multiple nuclei are also common, at least in the larger cities. However, though land use patterns are normally more complex than the sort of model outlined here would suggest, economists have sought to draw conclusions from the model concerning the efficiency of allocation achieved by a price system.

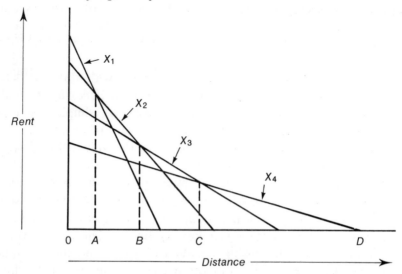

Figure 5.1   The allocation of land between competing uses

The general argument is as follows. The price system ensures that land is allocated between individual firms and households according to the amount each user is willing to pay for it. If this latter amount reflects the productivity of the land in each use, then the outcome is that the competing demands are reconciled in such a way that each piece of land is allocated to its most productive use. This proposition may be demonstrated in quite sophisticated ways. However, even at a simple level (or perhaps especially at a simple level!) the argument has considerable intuitive appeal. If each individual firm or household knows best which location is the most efficient, unregulated individual decision making would appear to lead to an ideal outcome. At the intra-urban level the geographical distribution of firms and households will reflect their relative needs for accessibility to the central area. At the regional level, factors of production will flow to where their productivity is highest: capital will flow to areas with a high return on capital investment whereas labour will flow to areas where its return is highest. Given that the returns to capital and labour reflect their relative productivities (as the orthodox marginal productivity theory of distribution would suggest), the spatial allocation of resources achieved through the price system results in maximum efficiency. As Richardson says, 'in perfect competition, the optimal regional allocation of resources maximises national output, and represents a Pareto optimum where it is impossible to increase the value of any output in one region without decreasing the value of some other output in another region'.[6]

Underlying Assumptions

The foregoing analysis is based on a number of quite restrictive assumptions. To the extent that these do not hold in practice, our confidence in the conclusions must be correspondingly diminished. The most important are as follows.

Assumption 1 The location of firms is determined by the profit maximisation criterion.

We noted in Chapter 3 that, as a general assumption in the theory of the firm, the profit maximisation postulate has been under much attack. Economists are divided on this matter. Some, such as Baumol, Williamson and Marris contend that other postulates (maximisation of sales revenue, discretionary expenditure or growth) may have more generality.[7] Others, including such 'strange bedfellows' as Machlup and Sweezy, argue that the quest for maximum profit remains the driving force of business activity.[8] The point here is that, even if profit maximisation is still the best assumption on which to base theories of business price and output policy, it is of more doubtful status as a basis for a theory of business location. As Richardson says, 'the assumption of economic rationality may be reasonable for most managerial decisions . . . but it is not necessarily justifiable when applied to the location decision'.[9] Chance and 'the early start' have long been recognised as important location influences, and recent empirical research also suggests that there are some relatively systematic characteristics of firms' decision-making. These do not support the maximising view so much as the 'satisficing' view. As I have argued

---

[6] H. W. Richardson, *Regional Economics*, London, Weidenfeld and Nicolson, 1969, p. 288.

[7] See W. Baumol, *Business Behaviour Value and Growth,* New York, Macmillan, 1959, O. E. Williamson, *The Economics of Discretionary Behaviour*, Englewood Cliffs N.J., Prentice-Hall, 1964, and R. Marris, *The Economic Theory of Managerial Capitalism*, London, Macmillan, 1964.

[8] See F. Machlup, Theories of the Firm: Marginalist, Behavioural, Managerial, *American Economic Review*, March 1967, pp. 1-33, and P. Baran and P. Sweezy, *Monopoly Capital*, Harmondsworth, Penguin Books, 1968, Chapter 2.

[9] H. W. Richardson, op. cit., p. 94.

elsewhere[10], the typical process has the following features:

(1) the location decision arises as the result of a near-crisis situation, such that a speedy decision is more important than an ideal decision;

(2) there is no systematic consideration of costs and revenues in alternative sites;

(3) especially in the case of branch plant locations, the tendency is to seek something suitable close at hand, the implicit assumption being that the present location is probably optimal.

Thus, rather than seek a location which is ideal, firms tend to select the first that passes some minimum satisfactory standard. Note too, that the standards are not necessarily purely economic ones either. In studying actual location decisions it is not rare to find that the managing director's wife plays an important role! The impact on the orthodox argument for unrestricted individual locational choice is fairly clear. A necessary condition for confidence in that argument is unfilled because it is no longer certain that resources will flow to where their economic return is highest.

Assumption 2   Perfect knowledge.

The orthodox theory assumes that location decisions are based on full information of the range of alternative sites and their attributes, including the costs and revenues associated with business activities. However, this requirement is not generally met. Indeed, part of the need for a satisficing approach arises from the imperfection of information. The satisficing firm does not even seek perfect knowledge but is content with a much more restricted information search procedure. The result is that firms themselves do not even know the likely effect on location of resource productivity. As Luttrell concluded after conducting a major study of manufacturing location in Britain, 'we should have liked to give an example of the classic location decision in which operating cost estimates were made for two or more possible places, all imponderables or non-cost factors assessed and then a way found of comparing the good and bad points of one place with those of the other. Unfortunately, we were not able to find such a case.'[11]

Assumption 3   Perfect mobility of resources.

In practice, there are various impediments to any non-spatial change of resource use, such as a change in occupation within the same organisation, but the introduction of the spatial dimension further intensifies this problem. Indeed, it may be argued that it is these very problems of resource immobility which give the spatial aspects of economic analysis their particular importance.

[10] F. J. B. Stilwell, *Regional Economic Policy*, London, Macmillan, 1972, Chapter 2.
[11] W. F. Luttrell, *Factory Location and Industrial Movement*, London, N.I.E.S.R., 1962.

Some of the main sources of immobility are listed by Richardson as follows: 'Distance may limit the movement of labour, and workers (and managerial personnel) may be immobile because of preferences for living in one region rather than another, ignorance of income-earning opportunities, migration costs and non-economic considerations. Capital may not flow freely because of imperfect knowledge on the part of investors, rigidities in the capital market and variations in regional tax structures. Natural resources are normally immobile and regional endowments may differ widely in quantity and quality.'[12] Given these rigidities—and some of them embody important social and cultural preferences—the price system may serve a valuable function as a means of increasing efficiency. However, the possibility of using economic analysis to demonstrate that *optimal* resource allocation will be achieved in a market economy is severely restricted in these circumstances.

Assumption 4 No external effects associated with local decisions.

Yes, it is the externalities problem once again! External effects have a spatial dimension inasmuch as the 'spillovers' on to society from individual decisions vary according to location. Consider the example of a developer building a block of offices or flats within a metropolitan area. The principal costs he must pay are those of acquiring the land and of erecting the building. He does not normally have to compensate neighbouring residents for their loss of view, for the extra noise and atmospheric pollution, or for the extra congestion in local streets and other local public facilities. Nor is the developer held accountable for the problems of deteriorating physical and social environment often associated with urban expansion. Because the costs paid by developers exclude these social costs, they systematically understate the real costs of urban development. The result is that too much takes place. The failure of the economy to internalise the external or 'spillover' effects of growth causes a systematic tendency towards resource misallocation. Further, to the extent that external diseconomies predominate in developments located in major metropolitan areas, there is a tendency for large cities to grow beyond their optimum size. The growth of above optimum-sized cities is a logical outcome of a capitalist system which fails to make developers pay the full costs they impose on society.

Assumption 5 Perfect competition.

This assumption is the most restrictive of all and, in some respects, subsumes earlier assumptions such as perfect information and perfect mobility. For the market system to be conducive to maximum allocative efficiency in the spatial

[12] H. W. Richardson, *Regional Economics,* London, Weidenfeld and Nicolson, 1969, p. 293.

framework, prices must be flexible and reflect costs in alternative locations. This is true of perfect competition but less likely in situations of oligopoly and monopoly. However, monopoly and oligopoly are the typical spatial market forms, because transport costs and indivisibility of capital equipment limit the number of firms operating in any market area.[13] In oligopolistic and monopolistic market structures, prices are determined by individual producers rather than by aggregate supply and demand. As such they may remain fixed for quite long periods of time, despite changes in demand and cost conditions. Prices thereby cease to play their full allocative role. Moreover, prices need not be in line with costs, for example, where prices charged for delivered goods are uniform for all consumers, irrespective of the delivery distance and transport costs involved.

The prevalence of oligopoly has a further consequence; the size of producing units relative to the total market means that the location of any one firm is crucially dependent on the location of other firms. A well-established model first developed by Hotelling[14] can be used to illustrate one set of consequences. This model applies to the special case of oligopoly known as duopoly, where there are only two sellers of the product in question. It is illustrated in *Figure 5.2*.

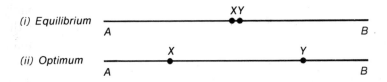

Figure 5.2   Location in a duopoly situation

Consider the linear market *AB* to be a beach along which slowly roasting sun-worshippers are fairly evenly distributed. If this market is served by one ice-cream seller (*X*), then he has a captive market and he can choose whichever location he pleases. Probably he will choose the centre, in which case the average distance of the customers to the seller is minimised, which is good for them as well as him. However, if another ice-cream seller (*Y*) moves in to the territory, where will he set up his stall? The answer is: also in the centre because then he gets exactly half the total market, assuming (a) that all consumers buy from the nearest seller and (b) no violence, (that is, that the previous seller

[13] Indeed, it has been argued that perfect competition is actually impossible in a spatially segmented market: see M. L. Greenhut, *A Theory of the Firm in Economic Space*, New York, Appleton-Century-Crofts, 1970, Chapter 4.

[14] H. Hotelling, Stability in Competition, *The Economic Journal*, Volume 34, 1929, pp. 41-57.

does not seek to protect his market by physically wiping out the potential competition!) The equilibrium is attained where they are located side-by-side at the centre of the market. If either moves away he gets less than half the market. However, this outcome is not in the consumers' interest. From their viewpoint the optimum would be where the two sellers are located at the quartiles, since then the average distance of each consumer from a seller is minimised.

This sort of analysis has been held to demonstrate the general tendency for spatial convergence in oligopolistic situations, and the tendency for such convergence to conflict with consumers' welfare. The model is actually rather simplistic, and the tendency for convergence is less obvious when more than two firms serve the market. Nevertheless, it provides an interesting illustration of the more general point that, when perfect competition does not prevail, the market will systematically violate criteria of allocative efficiency.

Equity Considerations

Orthodox economic theory is sometimes held to show that the spatial allocation of resources achieved by the price system is conducive to equity as well as efficiency. The central argument is that the use of a price system will ensure equalisation of the prices of the factors of production in each region. This proposition is in turn supported in a variety of different ways. Probably the best known 'proof' is that of Samuelson who sought to demonstrate that, in the absence of movements of factors of production, free trade would equalise prices. Trade is regarded as a mechanism by which commodity prices are equalised in all regions (or countries) and, given a unique relationship between commodity prices and factor prices, this leads to factor-price equalisation.[15] There are considerable problems with this analysis, not the least of which is that commodities produced in different regions are normally differentiated in some way, so that trade does not ensure the commodity-price equalisation which is a pre-condition for factor-price equalisation.

An alternative approach suggested by Mundell emphasises the role of factor movements rather than commodity movements.[16] The equilibrium process can be explained fairly simply. Consider two regions A and B, the former featuring a low return to labour but a high return to capital and the latter a high return to labour and a low return to capital. Labour can be expected to move from A to B, which will have the effect of raising its marginal productivity in the former and depressing it in the latter. Conversely, capital can be expected to

[15] P. A. Samuelson, International Trade and Equalisation of Factor Prices, *The Economic Journal*, Volume 58, 1948, pp. 163-184, and International Factor-Price Equalisation Once Again, *The Economic Journal*, Volume 59, 1949, pp. 181-197.

[16] R. A. Mundell, International Trade and Factor Mobility, *The American Economic Review*, Volume 47, 1957, 321-335.

flow from B to A, causing its marginal productivity to rise in B and fall in A. If mobility is perfect and is solely determined by economic considerations, then factor prices will be equalised in the two regions.

The last argument, while having a certain intuitive appeal, is subject to a number of limitations. Let us consider *labour* movement first. Most importantly, we cannot be sure that migration will occur on a sufficient scale. Most people have some locational inertia, arising because of social or cultural ties to the region in which they live. Even those people who have a fairly high propensity to move normally require more than a marginal adjustment in their potential income to induce them to migrate. Movement has its own costs in monetary as well as psychic terms.

Moreover, even if mobility is high, we cannot be sure that the result will be equilibrating. There are a number of reasons for this. Firstly, as commonly noted by development economists, migration flows are usually selective. It is the younger and more active people who move and, since these tend to become 'the entrepreneurs of tomorrow', their departure puts another nail in the economic coffin of the regions they leave. Secondly, the process of migration influences the distribution of demand in the economy as well as the distribution of labour supply. When people leave a region there is a reduction in the demand for goods and services, which has depressing effects on the local economy, especially if it is a fairly self-sufficient economy. On the other hand, a migration inflow leads to an increased demand which has expansionary effects on the economy of the host region. Thus, as Thirlwall has emphasised, migration of labour may tend to exaggerate regional problems by adding to expansionary pressures in regions with high wages and by causing further depressing effects in low wage regions.[17] The force of this argument depends on various empirical factors, such as the degree of excess capacity in infrastructure in the host region, the economic self-sufficiency of host and donor regions, the size of interregional remittances by migrant persons, and so on. Nevertheless, it does cast doubt on the generality of the assertion that mobility will result in interregional (and international) equity: in some circumstances it may have the reverse effect.

Similar arguments relate to the movement of *capital*. In practice, most of the existing capital stock is tied to particular locations: the only highly mobile components are funds for new investment. But even here there are problems, particularly those associated with risk and uncertainty. Capital may not flow to where its return is highest if risks are considered greater in regions which have featured low average rates of return in the past, even though the rate of return on new investment is higher than in other areas. This is likely to be

[17] A. P. Thirlwall, Migration and Regional Unemployment, *Westminster Bank Review*, November 1966, pp. 31-44.

accentuated where investment projects are large, in which case the applicability of orthodox marginal analysis becomes particularly dubious.

Finally, it should be noted that tendencies towards factor price-equalisation do not necessarily imply interregional equity anyway. A theory of factor prices is *not* a theory of distribution; the latter requires both a theory of factor prices and a theory of factor ownership. Various income distributions are consistent with any given set of factor prices. If the capital resources are owned by a small proportion of the population then the overall income distribution will tend to be more skewed than if their ownership is more evenly distributed. So, even *if* the price system tends to equalise factor prices in different regions, there is no reason to expect interregional equity.

Overall, it seems that the factor price-equalisation argument is somewhat of a red-herring. It is subject to much detailed criticism and seems founded on some rather dubious premises. Moreover, as the Swedish economist Myrdal notes, it flies in the face of observed reality at least so far as the international economy is concerned: 'We thus see the strange thing that in recent decades, while international economic inequalities have been growing and recently also become of more and more pressing concern in international politics, the theory of international trade has developed in the direction of stressing more and more the idea that trade initiates a tendency towards a gradual equalisation of factor prices and incomes as between countries'.[18]

Some Applications of the Analysis

This chapter concludes with some comments on the spatial distribution of economic activities, with particular reference to the problems associated with high degrees of urbanisation. Much attention has recently been given to the so-called 'urban crisis', but there is a strong and influential body of opinion which sees the market mechanism as capable of resolving the allocative problems involved. Implicit in this view are many of the assumptions which we have already examined earlier in this chapter. This concluding section seeks to contrast the conventional equilibrium view of spatial allocation with a quite different view.

It is quite clear that some degree of urbanisation is a necessary condition for industrial society. Historically, most countries have experienced urbanisation and industrialisation as two complementary elements. As Reissman notes 'with the rise of the factory, the city became necessary for economic reasons in a way that was not true before except for isolated examples . . . there was the need for many people to be in the city and to remain there more

---

[18] G. Myrdal, *Economic Theory and Underdeveloped Regions*, London, Methuen, 1957.

or less permanently'.[19] However, it is less clear why, even as nations move into a post-industrial phase, urbanisation continues just as relentlessly. There appears to be no turning back. Six of the major capitalist nations (Australia, Japan, West Germany, Denmark, the United States and Great Britain) now have 75 per cent or more of their population in urban areas.[20] Many others are not far behind. Metropolitan primacy—the situation where the domestic economy is dominated by a small number of major urban centres—is becoming the usual rather than the exceptional case. The People's Republic of China provides the principal example of an attempt to reverse the trend and to break down the distinction between city and country, but even there success has been limited.

It is difficult to explain this situation in terms of the conventional equilibrium analysis. This is not to say that it is impossible: it may be that metropolitan primacy reflects the tendency for the productivity of resources in urban areas to rise faster over time than that in rural areas. But such an explanation partly begs the question since it leaves the dynamics of productivity change unexplained. In studying such matters, static equilibrium models of the neo-classical type are less useful than the cumulative causation approach developed particularly through the work of Myrdal.[21] The great advantage of this approach to studying regional and urban growth is its ability to incorporate historical, geographical, political and social effects as well as purely economic considerations. The central notion is that of cumulative divergence between the prosperity of the urban centres and the predominantly rural peripheries. Once urban areas have developed to a certain size they tend to further increase their absolute and relative dominance at the expense of the areas which remain underdeveloped. Thus, although the reasons for their initial location may no longer be important (a resource since exhausted, a source of water now inadequate to serve local needs, and so on), the largest cities feature propulsive growth. The other areas, although potentially suitable for urban development, face relative stagnation.

According to this centre-periphery view, relationships between the metropolitan centres and the so-called peripheral regions, can be understood in terms of two conflicting forces, 'backwash' and 'spread' effects. The former lead to centralisation of growth and include the following:

---

[19] L. Reissman, *The Urban Process: Cities in Industrial Societies,* New York, Free Press of Glencoe, 1964.

[20] See T. van Dugteren, A Time to Decentralise, *Current Affairs Bulletin*, Sydney, December 1971.

[21] G. Myrdal, *Economic Theory and Underdeveloped Regions,* London, Methuen, 1957. See also A. O. Hirschman, *The Strategy of Economic Development,* New Haven, Yale University Press, 1959, and J. Friedmann, *Regional Development Policy*, Cambridge Mass., M.I.T. Press, 1966.

(1) large-scale economies in the use of social overhead capital, urban government and private business services;

(2) the advantage to industralists of access to a large labour market and to developed capital markets;

(3) the saving in transport costs in a relatively self-contained local economy;

(4) localisation economies due to the agglomeration of several firms within an industry;

(5) the failure of businessmen to perceive investment opportunities in non-metropolitan areas.

The list is not exhaustive. It could be extended, for example, by inclusion of considerations relating to the selective nature of migration mentioned earlier. Also there are political 'backwash' effects. One problem in this regard is the tendency for local government in the least well developed areas to be dominated by feudal-type power structures. Together with a general lack of resources for public sector expenditure, this tends to inhibit autonomous development in the peripheral regions. The most general point to be made about these 'backwash' effects is that, while some reflect a genuine economic advantage of the metropolitan centres, others do not. It is not only a question of externalities: cumulative causation reflects an inbuilt irrationality of the economic system, a process which would continue to occur even if more social costs were internalised within the price system.

The only checks to the growth of the centre at the expense of the periphery in a market economy are the 'spread' effects of urban growth. In part, these can be interpreted as the effect of scale diseconomies. Labour costs may become sufficiently low in non-metropolitan locations to encourage firms to decentralise their operations. Similarly, firms may seek to escape the adverse 'climate' of industrial relations in the urban environment, or the problems of traffic congestion which characterise the central area. However, such movement is usually fairly localised and is generally less than necessary to secure inter-regional equity. The information on which location decisions are based is usually very poor, especially when it concerns distant regions. Added to this is the naturally parochial outlook of decision makers and their frequently strong degree of risk-aversion. The result is that the 'spread' effects are usually very weak relative to 'backwash' effects.

Turning now to the consequences of this situation, there is no doubt that urbanisation conveys great advantages on large-scale industrialists. Rose argues that 'the advantages of an urban location for manufacturing are numerous. In the first instance, for the employer, location in a city is likely to ensure a wider and more skilled labour supply than could be commanded were the plant to be located in a rural area. . . . The country plant must meet most of the costs in finding its supply of water or electricity; it may have to pay the cost of transporting workers to and from the plant. In the city such costs are shared by the community at large. For the manufacturer, the city is likely to represent a substantial proportion of the total market for his wares. By locating his plant within the area he minimises the costs of shipping his product to market.'[22]

What of the employees? Business prosperity is usually regarded as one element in their welfare but the coincidence of interests is far from complete. To put it mildly, what is good for business is not *necessarily* good for the general population. There are certain advantages of urbanism: the range of available jobs is probably the most important single factor. There are also advantages in terms of access to places of entertainment, worship and so on.

To be set against these advantages are some important social disadvantages. Firstly, there is the impact of urbanisation on the quality of the physical environment. Greater spatial concentration of production and consumption activities increases the pollution problem by pushing pollution beyond the levels with which the natural waste disposal mechanisms in ecological systems can cope. Irreversible changes in ecological systems are precipitated which would not occur with less spatial concentration of the pollutive activities. Clearly, urbanisation itself is not the cause of the pollution problem, but it increases the difficulties of dealing with it.

A second set of disadvantages of urbanisation are the social problems associated with large cities: these include high crime rates and juvenile delin- quency, loneliness among elderly persons (and sometimes even the young), poor health, and the strains imposed by congestion on the roads, on public transport and in social facilities generally. Also, with increasing urban scale, travelling times increase so that less time is spent in the home, with conse- quent breakdowns in family and community life. This list could be extended to encompass many other social costs and, though it is important to distinguish between social problems *in* cities and social problems *of* cities, there is a growing volume of evidence on the caused links between urbanisation and problems of this kind.[23]

Thirdly, there is the effect of urbanisation on social inequality. This problem is receiving increasing attention, partly because the ethnic dimension of social inequality adds further to the resulting social tensions. It is not contended that urbanisation is the prime cause of inequality: that award clearly goes to the principle of private property ownership which underlies the capitalist

---

[22] A. J. Rose, *Patterns of Cities*, Melbourne, Thomas Nelson, 1967, p. 37.
[23] See F. J. B. Stilwell, *Australian Urban and Regional Development*, Sydney, ANZ, 1974, Chapters 10 and 11, and H. W. Richardson, *The Economics of Urban Size*, Farnborough, Saxon House, 1973, Chapter 8.

system. But large cities provide a further means by which inequality is accent-uated; as Stretton argues, 'very big cities are both physical and psycholog-ical devices for quietly shifting resources from poorer to richer, and for excusing or concealing—with a baffled but complacent air—the increasing deprivation of the poor'.[24] The pattern of land values in a large city would normally lead one to expect a spatial specialisation between areas where rich and poor persons live. This separation often provides a basis for further exploitation of the relatively poor groups, since public facilities are typically of a higher standard in the more wealthy areas. Moreover, because of the class character of suburbs the poor mix mainly with the poor and the rich with the rich, with the result that attitude differences are perpetuated and social mobility is diminished. In this way, the poor are socialised so as to accept their role more or less passively, and challenge to the existing political and economic order is minimised.

Other aspects of urbanisation could be mentioned and more documentation paraded. But this does not purport to be a comprehensive appraisal: rather the point is that urbanisation conveys certain advantages and disadvantages on certain sections of the community, and there is no reason to expect the outcome to be socially optimal in any general sense. On the contrary, the tendency towards cumulative divergence between the growth of metropolitan and peripheral regions, suggests that the problems are likely to intensify.

These difficulties are not limited to the capitalist nations. However, the possibility of breaking the vicious circle of cumulative causation is particularly problematic under this sort of system. It is normal in capitalist systems for development to be oriented towards the already most-developed sectors, since this is normally more profitable. As Gurley puts it: 'This pursuit of efficiency and private profits through building on the best has led in some areas to impressive aggregate growth rates, but almost everywhere in the international Capitalist world it has favoured only relatively few at the expense of the many, and, in poor Capitalist countries, it has left most in stagnant backwaters. Capitalist development, even when most successful, is always a trickle-down development.'[25]

[24] H. Stretton, *Ideas for Australian Cities*, Adelaide, Hugh Stretton, 1970, p. 310.
[25] J. Gurley, Capitalist and Maoist Economic Development, *Monthly Review*, February, 1971, p. 17.

CHAPTER SIX

When?

Most economic decisions involve considerations of time. For consumers, there is the recurrent choice between expenditure now and expenditure at a later date: how this decision is resolved determines the relative magnitude of consumption and saving. For young people making decisions about their careers, there is (sometimes) the choice between joining the workforce as soon as possible or spending time in further education or training in the hope of securing a more remunerative, prestigious or satisfying job later. For firms there are a variety of decisions involving time, including decisions about when to launch a new product, how to schedule ordering of inputs into productive processes, when to add to or diminish the level of stocks, and so on.

However, conventional economic theory treats considerations of time in an uncomfortable manner. The subject has both static and dynamic branches but, as far as the theory of resource allocation is concerned, the dynamic aspects are relatively poorly developed. The neo-classical analysis is largely an exercise in comparative statics. Time is treated in much the same way as in the body-building advertisements; one sees the 'before' and the 'after' but gains no insight into the process of change. Thus, rather than develop a new dynamic approach, economic theorists have tended to bring decisions involving time within the methodology of existing static analysis. This has imparted a particular flavour to the treatment of time. Let us look at how this applies to the analysis of consumer and producer behaviour.

Time and Consumers

A good example of attempts to reconstruct economic theory to incorporate time considerations is provided by the analysis of the consumer's choice between saving and consumption expenditure. Saving is the process of deferring consumption to a later date. In a simplified model where the consumer has a choice between consumption now and consumption later, the allocation of funds can be seen to depend principally on two matters, the rate of interest and the consumer's preferences as between consumption now and consumption later. Assume the person received income Y_1 in period 1 (the present) and expects to receive income Y_2 in period 2 (the future). The maximum consumption expenditure in period 1 is $Y_1 + Y_2/(1 + r)$ where r is the rate of interest. On the other hand the maximum consumption expenditure in period 2 is $Y_2 + Y_1 (1 + r)$, (assuming for simplicity that the rate of interest one pays on borrowed funds is the same as the rate one receives on loans).

This situation is illustrated *Figure 6.1*. The axes measure consumption expenditure in each period. The limit to the consumer's expenditure possibilities is shown by the line connecting $Y_1 + Y_2/(1 + r)$ and $Y_2 + Y_1 (1 + r)$ The combination of Y_1 and Y_2 is, of course, one point on this line. The ideal combination from the consumer's viewpoint can be identified once we introduce indifference curves showing the consumer's preferences between consumption now and consumption later. In the case illustrated, the consumer maximises his welfare by choosing the combination C_1 and C_2. This means that $Y_1 - C_1$ is saved in the first period and consumption expenditure in the second period is C_2 which is equal to $Y_2 + (Y_1 - C_1) (1 + r)$.

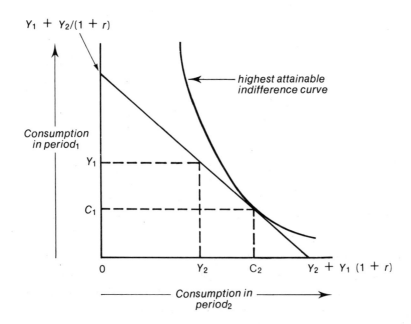

Figure 6.1   A two-period consumption analysis

This is a very simple model. It is used mainly to indicate that the conventional analysis is not completely incapable of handling decisions involving time. The real problem arises when the utility resulting from particular courses of action is not known. In some respects this reflects the general problem of lack of certainty which is not peculiar to decisions regarding intertemporal allocation; it arises whenever information about the consequences of alternative courses of action is incomplete. However, decisions involving time are particularly subject to this problem because of difficulties in the accurate prediction of future events. Some economists have responded by postulating that, rather than maximising utility at a given point of time, consumers seek to maximise *expected utility*. This provides a general criterion which is more useful than the conventional approach because it does recognise that complete certainty of outcome is the exception rather than the rule in consumption decisions. Even when the characteristics of the product being bought are fairly well-known, lack of certainty about the utility to be gained from it may still remain. However, the expected utility criterion is fully operational only in circumstances of measurable risk where probabilities can be attached to the alternative outcomes: it is much more difficult to apply in circumstances of uncertainty where the range and likelihood of possible outcomes and/or utilities associated with each are unknown. Being limited to circumstances of measurable risk makes the criterion a rather narrow one. Moreover, being based on the assumption that choice is consistently made to meet the demands of known and fixed tastes, leaves the criterion with important residual static elements. What if the consumers' objectives and tastes change over time, and adapt in the light of experience? What if the possibility of new products being introduced into the market is considered? In these circumstances our confidence that consumers' decisions result in maximisation of welfare is reduced. The process of utility maximisation is harder to sustain in the presence of limited information, uncertainty about the consequences of alternative courses of action and continually changing tastes.

Time and Producers

Similar attempts have been made to dynamise the orthodox economic theory of the firm. Static theory is based on the assumption that the firm maximises profits at a given point of time given particular cost and demand conditions. The dynamic theory sees the objective as the maximisation of the current value of an expected stream of profits over a period of time. As Needham puts it 'profit maximisation may be interpreted as a desire to maximise the present value of the profits expected from the firm's productive activities over a specific period'.[1] This provides a general criterion which economists have

---

[1] D. Needham, *Economic Analysis and Industrial Structure*, New York, Holt, Rinehart and Winston, 1969, p. 2.

attempted to use in understanding various aspects of business behaviour. Possibly its most important application is in terms of investment decisions, and it is with this aspect that much of the rest of this chapter is concerned.

Profit maximisation over time is normally seen as being achieved by the application of discounted cash flow (D.C.F.) methods of investment appraisal.[2] The general formula for evaluating the worth of any one investment project is as follows:

$$NPV = \frac{A_1}{1+r} + \frac{A_2}{(1+r)^2} + \frac{A_3}{(1+r)^3} + \ldots + \frac{A_n}{(1+r)^n}$$

Using a summation sign this can be condensed to:

$$NPV = \sum_{i=1}^{i=n} \frac{A_i}{(1+r)^i}$$

where: A_i is the estimated net cash inflow resulting from the project in the ith year;

n is the life of the project in years;

r is the rate of discount;

NPV is the net present value.

All projects with a positive NPV should be undertaken: all with a negative NPV should be rejected. (In the event of the projects being mutually exclusive only that with the highest NPV should be undertaken.) This is said to lead to long-run profit maximisation.[3]

Among other things, this approach emphasises the importance of opportunity costs. The cost of putting funds into one investment project is the return foregone by not putting those funds into another project. Thus, where the businessman's alternative to investing funds in his own firm is to loan those funds outside the firm, the appropriate rate of discount is the highest rate of interest that could be obtained on a loan with similar risk to the internal project. On the other hand, where the businessman has to borrow money in order to undertake the investment project, the alternative to undertaking the project is not to borrow the funds. In this case, the appropriate rate of discount is the rate of interest on borrowed funds.

---

[2] There are two principal variants of the D.C.F. approach, the internal rate of return method and the net present value method. The differences are relatively minor, and the discussion here centres on the latter method. For discussion of the relative merits of the two approaches, see any standard text on investment appraisal, such as H. Bierman and S. Smidt, *The Capital Budgeting Decision*, New York, Macmillan, 1960, Chapters 2 and 3.

[3] There is a minor problem associated with the timing of the cash inflows. The formula is strictly correct only if A_1 comes in one hit, a year after the time of decision and each subsequent inflow occurs at points of time separated by one year. If the flows are uneven during the year, inaccuracies in the application of the formula tend to set in.

This method of investment appraisal provides a useful method of choosing between alternatives with different time profiles. Generally speaking, it will reveal the economic superiority of projects which yield returns in early years over projects with similar aggregate returns spread over a larger number of years. This is consistent with the objective of profit maximisation because returns generated in early years can be re-invested in other projects.

However, the discounted cash flow approach has a number of limitations as a means of satisfactorily dealing with the time dimension. The most important difficulty arises because of the existence of risk and uncertainty. What if the decision maker is not certain about the magnitude and timing of the cash inflows resulting from a particular investment project? Then he has not the complete information needed to apply the D.C.F. formula. But, of course, this is the normal case; a businessman's knowledge of the factors which will determine the inflows associated with a particular investment some years hence is usually slight and often negligible. This means that the D.C.F. method must be adapted so that it is capable of handling situations of risk and uncertainty. Some suggestions have been put forward, including the use of sensitivity analysis, probability theory and of discount rates inflated by a risk factor.[4] By and large, these constitute modifications of the basic D.C.F. approach, although some scholars have also attempted to move away from the profit maximisation view of investment to a more general utility maximisation approach, involving subjective attitudes towards uncertainty.

There are a number of other more minor problems. The D.C.F. method is not generally applicable in situations where the investment proposals are interdependent. Also, particular difficulties arise in the situation of capital rationing, where the supply of funds for investment is restricted by means other than interest rates. However, generally speaking, economists have regarded the D.C.F. method as a principal means of introducing dynamic elements into the otherwise static theory of the firm. Thus, investment is regarded as the link between the short-run and the long-run, since it shows how those inputs which are fixed for the individual firm in the short-run can be varied in the long-run. In particular, the profit maximisation objective is shown to be capable of interpretation as a dynamic as well as a static decision rule.

Intertemporal Allocation and the Price System

We are now in a position to tackle a more explicitly normative question. What is the impact of inter-temporal consumption and investment decisions on community welfare? In particular, can we have any confidence in the market

---

[4] See H. Bierman and S. Smidt, *The Capital Budgeting Decision*, New York, Macmillan, 1960, chapters 11, 15 and 16.

mechanism as a means of ensuring that the intertemporal allocation of resources is consistent with community objectives? This is a very difficult issue. As we saw in Chapter 4, it is hard enough to deal with the concept of community objectives at a given point of time, let alone over time as changes occur in the individual objectives of its members (and often its membership too).

Orthodox economists have responded to the problem mainly by ignoring it. Very little attention is paid to the intertemporal problem in most books on microeconomics and welfare economics. The one aspect which has received some attention (more from applied economists working in cost-benefit analysis and the study of nationalised industries than from micro-theorists) concerns the relationship between the rate of discount used in making individual decisions about intertemporal allocation and the rate of discount applicable to the community as a whole. This latter variable is known as the *social rate of discount*: it indicates the weight given by the community to consumption at different points of time.

We saw earlier that individual consumers can be expected to apply a rate of discount in their choice between expenditure now (consumption), and expenditure later (saving). This rate depends on the rate of interest at which money can be borrowed and loaned. Similarly, businessmen making investment decisions with reference to the D.C.F. method must choose a rate at which to discount estimated future earnings; given the objective of profit maximisation, this decision will reflect the opportunity cost of using the funds in the particular project under consideration.

The question which arises now is whether there is any systematic deviation between these rates of discount used by consumers and producers and the ideal social rate of discount for the community as a whole.

The private rate of discount is largely determined in the market, according to the amount of funds which people are prepared to lend and borrow at different rates of interest. As such it reflects individuals' expression of time preference. This is not necessarily the same as the time preference of the society as a whole. As we shall see, there are various reasons for this, including considerations of risk, irreversibility of investment decisions, external effects, and so on. The result is that we cannot be certain that the market economy produces an optimal allocation of resources over time. That said, it should be stressed that critics of reliance on the market mechanism are far from united. In general they divide into two groups:

(1) those who argue that the social rate of discount is normally less than the private rate of discount;

(2) those who argue that the social rate of discount is normally greater than the private rate of discount.

This is not an arid debate. On the contrary, as Winch argues, it 'goes to the very root of the value premises on which welfare economics is based'.[5] Moreover, it has great implications for attitudes towards the capitalist system as a whole, and its ability to generate an appropriate rate of economic growth. Put in simple terms, those who adopt the first of the above stances normally contend that the market economy will not generate sufficient investment, whereas those who adopt the second stance contend that it generates too much. And, since investment is an important determinant of the rate of growth[6], one's stance in this matter determines one's attitude to growth under capitalism (or, more typically, one's attitude to growth under capitalism determines one's stance in this matter!).

Let us consider the two sets of arguments in more detail, beginning with the argument that intertemporal resource allocation in a market economy tends to be too present-oriented.

Not Enough Investment!

Why should we expect the rate at which individual consumers and producers discount future earnings to be greater than that which society as a whole would wish to apply? Cutting through to the essentials of what often appears to be a very technical issue, there seem to be at least four fairly distinct reasons why the private rate of discount can be expected to exceed the social rate of discount:

Death   It has been noticed that people die (!). One consequence of this is that individuals tend to discount the future quite highly. Because life is short (or perhaps more importantly) of uncertain length, one can never be sure that one will live long enough to enjoy a postponed benefit. Moreover, even if one does last long enough, one may be too old to enjoy it. But these problems do not apply to society as a whole: barring nuclear calamity, the community cannot be expected to die in the foreseeable future. Generations overlap. The postponed benefits of the present *will* be enjoyed by the community, though perhaps not by any individuals now living. Thus, it is argued that the social rate of discount is normally less than the private rate of discount.

---

[5] D. Winch, *Analytical Welfare Economics,* Harmondsworth, Penguin Books, 1971, p. 168.

[6] Investment, being one of the most volatile components of national income, plays a crucial role in determining the level of economic activity in capitalist economies. However, its importance in long-run economic growth should not be over-estimated. One empirical investigation suggests that only 13 per cent of growth of national income in the United States over the period 1950-62 could be attributed to growth in 'non-residential structures and equipment', compared with 27 per cent from growth of employment and 23 per cent from advances in knowledge. The corresponding figures for Northwest Europe were 14 per cent, 18 per cent and 16 per cent respectively: see E. F. Denison, *Why Growth Rates Differ*, Washington, D.C., The Brookings Institution, 1967.

Risk A rather similar aspect of the case for a low social rate of discount relates to the fact that the riskiness of any investment project is normally higher for the individual investor than for society as a whole. For example, five firms in an oligopolistic market may be separately considering investment in some particular research and development project. Each firm may consider the venture highly risky but, for the industry as a whole, the risk is much smaller. It is possible, for example, that one firm could undertake the research project, but that eventually all would benefit from the outcome: patent rights provide only a temporary impediment in such circumstances. Thus, it is argued, individual risk is greater than social risk, because, though an individual may not receive all the benefits from an investment project, society continues to do so.

Impatience A third reason for having a low social rate of discount has been attributed to individuals' propensity to impatience. Rothenburg defines this as 'a situation in which the individual when he acts upon his short-run preferences acts inadvertently with respect to time in terms of his long-run preferences'.[7] Such impatience may be due to a variety of factors, but the important point is that it leads to intertemporal decisions which are not even in an individual's own self-interest, let alone the interests of future generations. Knowing of his propensity to impatience, the individual can be expected to seek to delegate power to the government to act in a corrective way. Thus, it is argued, individuals acting collectively will use a lower rate of discount than in their private consumption and investment decisions.

Altruism Finally, there is a special argument which has been put forward by Marglin in support of a low social rate of discount.[8] It is based on each individual having a general concern for the welfare of subsequent generations. Such altruistic motives would normally lead him or her to advocate a higher level of investment. However, each individual will feel that the investment should be undertaken by others of the current generation, not himself or herself. (Altruism doesn't stretch that far!) In these circumstances, it is argued that collective action provides the solution. Additional investment might be considered worthwhile by all acting together, though each person acting individually would not undertake it. In such a case the social rate of discount would be below the private rate of discount.

Each of these arguments is subject to qualification, but together they are quite persuasive.

[7] J. Rothenburg, *An Approach to the Welfare Analysis of Intertemporal Resource Allocation*, Athens, Center of Planning and Economic Research, 1967, p. 43.

[8] S. Marglin, The Social Rate of Discount and the Optimal Rate of Investment, *The Quarterly Journal of Economics,* February, 1963, pp. 95-111.

Too Much Investment!

A second school of thought is that the social rate of discount is greater than the private rate of discount and, as a consequence, the operation of a market economy results in a rate of capital accumulation which is too high. The main argument relates to the external effects associated with investment decisions. It is argued that such 'spillovers' are largely negative, causing a reduction in economic welfare. These negative spillovers can be separated into physical and social environmental effects. We consider each in turn.

Quality of the physical environment   Concern with the impact of a high level of investment on the quality of the environment is not new but it has recently intensified in a quite dramatic manner. This is particularly attributable to two major studies published in 1972, *The Limits to Growth* and *Blueprint for Survival*. The former was the result of a study sponsored by the Club of Rome and conducted at the Massachusetts Institute of Technology. It argued the need for a deliberate controlled end to growth which would otherwise exhaust many world resources and result in ecological catastrophe.[9] The latter was produced by thirty-three scientists and their general conclusion was similar, that 'if current trends are allowed to persist the breakdown of society and the irreversible destruction of life-support systems on the planet . . . are inevitable'.[10]

There is a continuing controversy about the methodology of these researchers, the imminence of the problem, and about possible ways of avoiding (or, at least, postponing) the crisis. One group, of whom the most eloquent is Paul Erlich, puts most emphasis on control of population growth. Another view (and one not entirely distinct from the first) puts most emphasis on investment and economic growth; a reduction in the rate of growth is seen as a necessary condition in the light of the growing environmental problem. Others emphasise the problems associated with the particular form which economic growth has taken.

It is in this last respect that the concept of external effects is particularly relevant. The environmental deterioration consequent on business investment decisions is an external effect because the investing firm does not usually have to compensate the community for the deterioration following from its decision. Thus, unless firms act in a directly benevolent rather than profit maximising manner, or unless the price system is modified so as to internalise these costs, business decisions will systematically violate environmental goals. A capitalist system in which environmental costs are external to the market is necessarily one of deteriorating environment. Air and water are 'free goods'

[9]   D. L. Meadows et. al., *The Limits of Growth*, New York, Universe Books, 1972.
[10]   Blueprint for Survival, supplement to *The Ecologist*, 1972.

to the individual producer or consumer. They fall outside the market system. It is hardly surprising that they are used whenever it is possible to increase profits by doing so. They are particularly useful as cheap and convenient receptacles for waste emissions. The result is a high level of pollution.

Added to this is the problem that many economic actions have *irreversible* consequences for environmental quality. Mining of minerals is an obvious case in point, particularly where it takes the form of open-cast mining: although areas *may* be revegetated (they often aren't) their ecological structure is usually irreversibly destroyed. On a less obvious level, pollution of air and water may lead to important irreversibilities. For example, part of the opposition to supersonic passenger aircraft like the Anglo-French Concorde, is because of the potential effects of ozone concentrations on the upper atmosphere. We simply do not know the ecological consequences of so many matters of this type. To continue to forge ahead with such investments would therefore appear to be in violation of environmental considerations. Even if only *some* of the ecological consequences turn out to be irreversible, the result is, at least, undesirable from the viewpoint of future generations or, at worst, disastrous.

Quality of the social environment   The second main strand of argument for a lower level of investment concerns the *social* consequences of a society based on advanced technology. It is argued that capitalism, because of its emphasis on material values, encourages the use of a form of technology which is inconsistent with many social objectives. To some extent this argument begs the question of how social values are identified (a question which we looked at earlier in Chapter 4). However, there seems to be a general widening of the concern with the social consequences of investment in economic growth which is oriented towards capital-intensive technology. Mishan's *The Costs of Economic Growth* is probably the most important contribution from an economist on this subject. The book is quite conservative in many ways; for example, it summarily dismisses income redistribution policies in three pages and puts considerable weight on solutions like 'separate facilities' which widen the scope for social segregation while doing little of direct value to improve the lot of the poorest section of the community. However, it does raise many important issues which economists have often tended to neglect.[11]

Some of the social problems linked with a high rate of economic growth (and, hence, indirectly with the investment resulting from the application of an undesirably low rate of discount) are as follows:

(1)   the alienation associated with employment in an economy based on complex industrial technology;

[11]   E. J. Mishan, *The Costs of Economic Growth*, Harmondsworth, Penguin Books, 1969.

(2)   the personal problem of adjustment to ever changing forms of social organisation;[12]

(3)   the growing problem of noise pollution, particularly associated with the heavy emphasis on motor transport and on the continual physical restructuring of the cities;

(4)   the reduction in cultural diversity as architecture, literature, and so on becomes increasingly similar the world over;

(5)   the spread of larger and larger metropolitan areas which offer a more and more harried existence as more and more time must be spent in travelling;

(6)   an increase in the anonymity of individuals, who become more and more dwarfed by the large-scale organisations which modern technology demands;

(7)   a decrease in the quality of consumers' decisions as they are faced with a baffling array of alternatives, so baffling, some argue, that further extensions of choice reduce welfare.

Many of these social problems arise from the particular direction which economic growth has taken. Like the physical environmental costs, these social problems arise largely because they are 'external' to the decision processes which cause them to arise. By and large, there is no need for firms to take account of the long-run social consequences of their investment decisions. Because these social costs do not bear directly on the calculus of profit and loss, degradation of the social environment can be expected to be a systematic phenomenon.

A Reconciliation?

It is now time to strike some sort of balance. We have examined two sets of arguments; one suggests that the form and level of investment is non-optimal because investment decisions are based on a too-high rate of discount; the others suggest that the form and level of investment is non-optimal because investment decisions are based on a too-low rate of discount. These arguments might appear to be diametrically opposed. However, they have a similar flavour in that they both suggest that the capitalist system is unable to guarantee the 'right' decisions about allocation of resources over time. Moreover, there is a possible reconciliation. This is related to the Galbraithian argument about 'social balance' first considered in Chapter 4. There is too much investment in particular types of economic activities and too little in others. In the former

[12] This point has been taken up most enthusiastically in A. Toffler, *Future Shock*, London, Pan Books, 1971.

category come all activities with 'negative spillovers' either for the physical or social environment. In the latter category come those activities from which future generations could be expected to benefit, for example, investment in education, medical research, conservation, and so on. So we can see that the problem of social balance has an important intertemporal dimension. Indeed, it can be said that what we have been looking at in the last few pages is the intertemporal dimension of the problem of social balance.

Some Macro-economic Applications

The sort of arguments we have been examining in this chapter have been used to rationalise particular macro-economic policies. Most importantly, they have been applied to the debate about policies to stimulate economic growth.

Most orthodox economists argue that the case for faster economic growth is strong and, indeed, almost self-evident. This, as Mishan notes: 'though no economist who has studied the relation between economics and social welfare would endorse a policy of economic growth without an embarrassing amount of qualification, the profession behaves as if, on balance, it is a good thing'.[13] Therefore, much attention is given to means by which economic growth can be accelerated, and it is here that the government—by labour retraining programmes, manpower planning, investment subsidies, immigration programmes, and so on—is seen as playing a major role.

The pro-growth viewpoint is supported by arguments of differing sophistication. Specific reference is sometimes made to the conflict between private and social discount rates. More commonly, faster growth is justified as widening the range of social choice. Thus, Arthur Lewis argues that 'the case for economic growth is that it gives man greater control over his environment and thereby increases his freedom'.[14] The argument is often debased—Parish, for example, *defines* economic growth as 'greater capacity to do what we would wish to do'[15] (so how could you not be in favour of it?). However, the general proposition has much appeal, particularly when applied to the countries of the 'third world' and to the less prosperous regions of the more affluent nations.

Certainly, it is true that the case for a faster rate of economic growth has been repeated almost *ad nauseam* in official government policy statements. The United States provides the most obvious example. As Passell and Ross note, during the 1960's in particular, 'stepped-up economic growth was the

[13] E. J. Mishan, *The Costs of Economic Growth*, Harmondsworth, Penguin Books, 1969, p. 62.
[14] W. A. Lewis, *The Theory of Economic Growth*, London, Allen and Unwin, 1955, p. 421.
[15] R. M. Parish, Economic Aspects of Pollution Control, *Economic Papers*: No. 38, October, 1971.

official and uncontested aim of national policy' (though Passell and Ross further argue that in practice this objective was 'sacrificed to the classic myths of economic orthodoxy—the virtues of unchanging prices, balanced budgets, and international exchange stability').[16] In Great Britain, the establishment of the National Economic Development Council in 1962 was widely seen as an attempt to *institutionalise* the growth objective. The National Plan, produced by the Department of Economic Affairs and published in 1965 began with the words, 'This is a plan to provide the basis for greater economic growth'.[17] Similarly, in Australia, the Vernon Report, the most influential document on economic management in the post-war period described growth as 'the central objective to which all other stated objectives should be related' and quoted approvingly the remark of Adam Smith to the effect that 'the progressive state is in reality the cheerful and hearty state to all the difference orders of society. The stationary is dull; the declining melancholy.'[18]

In recent years the increased attention drawn to the adverse physical and social 'spillovers' of economic growth has somewhat undermined the legitimacy of the pro-growth orthodoxy. However, the effect should not be exaggerated. In terms of its impact on government policy the achievements of the anti-growth faction have been extremely limited. Indeed, it has been strongly argued that the viability of the capitalist system depends on the maintenance of a high rate of economic growth. Its continued prosperity—and indeed its continued existence—depends on the government acting to accelerate growth. We conclude this chapter with a consideration of this important argument.

Since the writings of Keynes in the 1930's, orthodox economists have recognised that there is no tendency for full employment under capitalism. (It was actually recognised long before that by the millions of persons who were unemployed!) If there is one thing on which orthodox economists agree it is that, in the absence of government policy, the economy would be characterised by periodic depression. However, some economists go further than this and argue that the problem of potential depression is actually getting worse over time. The economic surplus—defined in simple terms by Baran and Sweezy as 'the difference between what society produces and the costs of producing it'—is growing over time.[19] This surplus must be absorbed or else

---

[16] P. Passell and L. Ross, *The Retreat from Riches*, New York, The Viking Press, 1971, pp. 91 and 115.

[17] Department of Economic Affairs, *The National Plan*, London, HMSO, 1965, p. 1.

[18] *Report of the Committee of Economic Enquiry*, (The Vernon Report), Canberra, Commonwealth of Australia, 1965, p. 28.

[19] The size of the surplus in the United States is estimated by Phillips as having risen from 46.9 per cent of Gross National Produce in 1929 to 56.1 in 1963: see P. Baran and P. Sweezy, *Monopoly Capital*, Harmondsworth, Penguin Books, 1968, p. 374.

aggregate production must be curtailed, leading to declining incomes and unemployment (and possibly political action to overthrow the capitalist system). The means of surplus absorption include:

(1) capitalist's own consumption and investment;
(2) the sales effort: advertising and other sales promotion activities designed to stimulate consumers' demand above the level at which it would otherwise stabilise;
(3) civilian government expenditure: the provision of public education, roads, police, health services, legislatures, administrators and so on;
(4) military expenditure.

Of these four means of absorbing the surplus and thereby maintaining the stability of the capitalist system, the last two lie clearly within the province of the government. Baran and Sweezy regard military expenditure as particularly important. They say that 'the big question . . . is not whether there will be more and more government spending, but on what. And here private interests come into their own as a controlling factor. . . . It is of course in the area of defence purchases that most of the expansion has taken place.'[20] Heilbroner agrees: 'a central aspect of our growth experience of the past two decades is . . . the fact that our great boom did not begin until the onset of the Second World War and that its continuance since then has consistently been tied to a military rather than to a purely civilian economic demand'.[21]

The reason for government intervention to accelerate economic growth in the capitalist system now becomes clearer. Such intervention is a necessary condition for the continued existence of the system. In these circumstances it is unrealistic to expect the anti-growth arguments to have much impact on government policy towards growth. Some concessions can be expected and, indeed, some sectors of the economy (for example, the production of anti-pollution devices of various forms) may actually profit as a result of incremental environment policies. However, where environmental aims conflict with the maintenance of the high level of material output on which the viability of the capitalist system depends, environmental objectives will normally be the ones which are sacrificed.

[20] P. Baran and P. Sweezy, *Monopoly Capital*, Harmondsworth, Penguin Books, 1968, p. 153 and 155.
[21] R. Heilbroner, *The Future as History*, New York, Harper & Row, 1960, p. 133.

CHAPTER SEVEN

Public Policy

It is now time to pull some strands together and look at the political implications of the discussion. We have been looking at the economic theory of resource allocation and some of the arguments for and against the price system as an allocative device. Generally the approach has been very critical. The central theme has been that even the models normally forwarded by mainstream economists to support reliance on the price system fail to provide a comprehensive intellectual underpinning for the market system. The various criticisms which have been mentioned are a rather mixed bag. Now it is time to arrange them in a more systematic framework and consider their full implications.

It is particularly important to distinguish between liberal and radical criticisms. The essential difference is a political one. Liberal economists are often critical of the orthodox neo-classical theory and of particular aspects of the capitalist system, but they see the solution in reform; reform of economic theory and reform of the economic system. Radicals, on the other hand, adopt a stronger position; they argue that revolutionary change is needed, both in the structure of economic analysis and in the economic system which that economic theory seeks to legitimise.

The liberal view is treated in this chapter, and the radical view in the next.

Liberal Economic Ideology

Historically, the growth of liberal ideology coincides with the industrial transformations of the eighteenth and nineteenth century. (Indeed, some argue that it was a necessary accompaniment.) This was the period of classical liberal thought, characterised by the writings of scholars such as Hobbes, Locke and Bentham. Hunt identifies the four basic assumptions of this school as those of:

(1) *egoism*: all human motivation is assumed to be selfish;
(2) *intellectualism*: individuals are assumed to take rational decisions of the basis of calculations about the pleasure and pains involved in alternative courses of action;

(3) *inertia*: individuals are assumed to stir from their natural state of laziness only when specific incentives are offered;

(4) *atomism*: the individual is considered to be a more fundamental reality than the group or society.[1]

These assumptions later became the basis on which the neo-classical theory of consumption and production were erected. The individual is the centre of theorising and he is seen as a utility-maximiser, his utility being positively related to the quantities of commodities (the only source of pleasure?) consumed and negatively related to the amount of work (always a source of pain?) undertaken. Business behaviour is also interpreted in this individualistic framework: profits are the variable to be maximised because they are the source of consumption expenditure for the owner. The many consumers and producers interact in the market, establishing a general equilibrium where prices serve the function of allocating the scarce resources among the competing parties.

This view of the economic system also relied heavily on the form which scientific progress had taken in other fields. The influence of Newton's work in the physical sciences is sometimes held to be particularly important. The basic concept of Newtonian physics is that of an atomistic world governed by immutable laws of motion. The concept of equilibrium is of central importance, and progress in science is envisaged as a process of increasing the understanding of the mechanics by which equilibrium is attained. The association between equilibrium and optimum, though seldom stated, is certainly implied. A similar viewpoint came to dominate enquiry in the social sciences. 'The eighteenth century viewed social forms as fixed in nature and what social change took place was at most a quantitative one set by the natural order of things. The universe was a mechanical piece often likened to a clock whose moving parts, when once wound up by a divine Creator, would run eternally in the same pre-established mechanical arrangement.'[2] Adam Smith's *The Wealth of Nations* can be regarded as the embodiment of this view. In place of Newton's law of gravitation, Smith substituted 'self-interest'. The result was a view of society in which each individual, by exercising his or her natural right to act in a purely self-interested manner, would promote the collective interest. Such a view provided an apparent legitimacy for the 'free enterprise' system and set the framework within which subsequent economic thought developed.

A further influence on economic ideology derived from Darwin's work on the theory of evolution. As Hofstadter recounts, 'thinkers of the Darwinian era seized upon the new theory and attempted to sound its meaning for the several social disciplines . . . (and) the conclusions to which Darwinism were

[1] E. K. Hunt, *Property and Prophets*, New York, Harper and Row, 1972, Chapter 4.
[2] D. Hamilton, *Evolutionary Economics*, Albuquerque, New Mexico U.P. 1970, p. 19.

first put were conservative solutions. . . . The most popular catchwords of Darwinism, "struggle for existence" and "survival of the fittest", when applied to the life of man in society, suggested that nature would provide that the best competitors in a competitive situation would win, and that this process would lead to a continuing improvement.'[3] Darwin himself objected to this application of his theory but the influence of social Darwinists has been significant (though its consequences for the structure of economic analysis are less obvious than those of Newtonian physics).

Liberals have sometimes sought to disassociate themselves from conservatives, especially those in the social Darwinist tradition. However, the division is not clear. The main difference between liberals and conservatives in practice lies in the extent to which they consider this concept of an economic system to be subject to practical flaws. Whereas conservatives see few, liberals see many. Thus, liberals usually advocate quite extensive government intervention. As Gordon argues, 'the two perspectives differ sharply on what should be done about such problems. And this difference draws essentially from their respective analyses of the State. In the liberal view, the State in a modern democracy adequately reflects individual wishes through group representatives. The government is justified in acting, essentially, because it incorporates the preferences of all individuals and because it seeks to advance the interests of all individuals. . . . In the conservative view, the role of the State should be much more limited. Conservatives tend to have greater faith than liberals in the efficiency and optimality of the private market mechanism, and to have greater fear than liberals of both government inefficiency and government infringement on personal liberties.'[4] However, it should be strongly stressed that, though they are in favour of *ad hoc* intervention, liberals still generally adhere to the belief in a free-enterprise economic system based primarily on the private ownership of property.

The rest of the current chapter considers various problems that liberals recognise in relation to market economies, and the public policies which they typically argue that governments should introduce to correct them.

Failure to establish 'ideal' conditions

The first set of problems arises from real world 'imperfections' which cause resource allocation to deviate from that of the 'ideal'. These 'imperfections' include the existence of monopoly and other 'imperfect' market structures, resource immobility, and consumer irrationality in the presence of biased

[3] R. Hofstadter, *Social Darwinism in American Thought*, Boston, Beacon Press, 1959.

[4] D. M. Gordon, *Problems in Political Economy: An Urban Perspective*, New York, D. C. Heath, 1971, pp. 10-11.

commercial advertising. Such things all reduce the applicability of the neo-classical models based on the assumptions of perfect competition, perfect mobility and perfect knowledge.

(a) Let us consider the *perfect competition* assumption first. This has had a particularly important role in the development of economic theory. It can be argued that it was never intended to provide a description of actual market structures, but economists have clung to it because of its analytical simplicity. Also it has fulfilled an ideological function in that it has served to provide an apparent justification for private enterprise from the viewpoint of allocative efficiency. Some have even argued that, because the perfect competition model excludes consideration of monopoly profits, it implies a less inequitable distribution than is actually experienced. Such points may help it explain its continued acceptance by conservative and liberal economists.

The problem is that the necessary requirements for perfect competition are so restrictive as to make the model quite unworkable in practice. Competition between firms often leads to a diminution of the number of the contestants as the strong crush or absorb the weak. Much enterprise goes into attempts to restrict the entry of new firms because it is quickly realised that this is what makes high profits of an otherwise temporary nature. Added to this, changing technology favours the concentration of production in larger firms. The result is the growth of monopoly and oligopoly and of a whole range of business strategies designed to keep prices above the competitive level. We noted in Chapter 4 that this normally leads to problems of allocative inefficiency. The quantitative importance of such inefficiency is not clear; Harberger, for example, contends that it is relatively minor.[5] Other economists have argued that the sacrifice of some allocative efficiency is a small price to pay for the higher rate of innovation which is associated with oligopoly. However, this view is difficult to support. After reviewing the existing evidence, Mansfield concludes that 'contrary to the allegations of Galbraith, Schumpeter and others, there is little evidence that industrial giants are needed in all or even most industries to promote rapid technological change and rapid utilisation of new techniques'.[6]

In practice, liberals almost invariably proceed on the assumption that public policies to increase competition are needed. In part this appears to reflect a fundamental belief in the ideal properties of the perfectly competitive model, and a belief (mistaken as we shall see later) that the closer we can approximate to it the better. In part it also reflects the more clearly political

[5] A. C. Harberger, Monopoly and Resource Allocation, *The American Economic Review*, Papers and Proceedings, Volume 64, 1954, pp. 77-87.
[6] E. Mansfield, *Microeconomics*, New York, Norton, 1970, p. 465.

objective of preventing great accretions of economic power which can be used for socio-political ends. Better many small wolves than one big bad wolf! Thus, liberal policy towards industrial organisation typically takes the form either of measures to prevent the worst abuses of monopoly power or to establish 'workable competition'. The former involves policies to limit the conduct of firms in concentrated industries, such as restrictive practices legislation or maximum price legislation. The latter approach is more explicitly concerned with industrial structure and may involve policies to restrict mergers, to break up existing large firms into smaller units, or even the establishment of state-owned firms to compete with the existing private enterprise firms. Most developed capitalist nations have introduced such measures though with varying consistency and degrees of vigour. Economists disagree on the success of such policies but, in relation to industrial concentration, the policies seem to have been greatly outweighed by the forces of agglomeration. There is plentiful evidence that concentration has been increasing over time in most advanced capitalist nations. This is particularly important in the light of empirical findings on the relationship between profitability, concentration and restrictions on the entry of new firms. As Mann notes 'industries with high concentration ratios and high barriers to entry appear to be at the core of any resource misallocation due to monopolistic prices'.[7]

(b)   The second necessary condition to ensure optimal resource allocation in a market economy is that of *perfect mobility*. Again this is manifestly unrealistic as a description of the society in which we live; indeed there is some reason to believe that it is becoming increasingly unrealistic. This may occasion some surprise: after all, great technological advances in transport and communications have broken down many of the constraints of geography. However, when it comes to occupational mobility, it seems that this same technological change, by increasing the specialisation of function, creates growing problems of immobility.

   Liberals generally recognise this problem but argue that its severity can be reduced through public policies of various sorts. While it is realised that, like perfect competition, perfect mobility is an unattainable ideal, measures to increase mobility are often quite vigorously pursued. This is particularly true of geographical mobility. The liberal attitude to regional problems is typically one of 'lubricating' the market mechanisms which lead resources to flow to where their returns are highest. Labour in particular is encouraged to be geographically mobile, often at quite considerable social cost in terms

---

[7] H. M. Mann, Seller Concentration, Barriers to Entry and Rates of Return in Thirty Industries, 1950-1960, *The Review of Economics and Statistics*, August 1966, pp. 296-307.

of the disruption of families and communities and the reduction in inter-regional cultural variation. In relation to occupational mobility, liberals sometimes advocate the establishment of government-sponsored retraining centres in which the victims of technological change can seek to acquire new skills. More generally, liberals look to the educational system for the solution to occupational immobility and advocate more education as a means of in-creasing the flexibility of the workforce. In so doing they often ignore the tendency for the benefits of expanded educational systems to accrue mainly to those from the most privileged backgrounds. Also, as the sociologist Theodore Caplow argues, 'the principal device for limitation of occupational choice is the education system. It does this in two ways: first, by forcing the student who embarks upon a long course of training to renounce other careers which also require extensive training: second, by excluding from training and eventually from the occupations themselves those students who lack either the intellectual qualities (such as intelligence, docility, aptitude) or the social characteristics (such as ethnic background, wealth, appropriate conduct, previous education) which happen to be required.'[8]

(c)   As for the assumption of *perfect knowledge*, this is clearly also invalid. But is there *sufficient* information for the making of reasonably rational de-cisions? Certainly, a large volume of resources is devoted to the provision of information through advertising and sales promotion activities. However, some of it is seriously misleading, and nearly all of it is biased. Moreover, to the extent that a growing volume of commercial advertising adds to consumer bamboozlement rather than consumer enlightenment, it leads to a lower quality of consumers' decisions. As Mishan says, 'the task of choosing in a rational way, on each occasion, one brand or model from a bewildering and, indeed, ever changing array of such goods—that is, to weigh up the relative merits of quality, taste, appearance, performance, longevity, and other charac-teristics with respect to the range of prices of some several score objects all purporting to serve the same need—would be too time-consuming and too exhausting an occupation even if the entire staff of a Consumers' Advisory Board were placed at the customer's disposal'.[9] The most plausible conse-quence of this situation is a declining rationality of decision making.

The liberal response is rather varied. At the conservative end of the spectrum there is the argument of Johnson that 'advertising is one aspect of the eco-nomics of information' and that 'advertising as we know it represents an

[8] T. Caplow, *The Sociology of Work*, Minneapolis, 1954, p. 216, quoted in R. C. Edwards, M. Reich and T. E. Weisskopf (Eds.), *The Capitalist System*, Englewood Cliffs, New Jersey, 1972, p. 232.
[9] E. J. Mishan, *The Costs of Economic Growth*, Harmondsworth, Penguin Books, 1969, p. 157.

accommodation by market competition between the kind of informational messages that consumers would like to have and the kind of effective selling messages that producers find it most economical to communicate given the technology of the communications industry'.[10] Economists sharing this sort of view normally limit themselves to arguing for control on deceitful advertising claims. Others go further and argue for a tax on commercial advertising expenditure. This can be justified on various grounds, but generally reflects the liberal belief in maintaining the freedom of the producer to advertise while seeking to internalise the negative spillovers of that activity. Mishan goes further still. His solution involves the public sector taking over the role of providing information to consumers. 'All that which is relevant in enabling the public to make a rational choice from the range of material goods and services offered by private enterprise may be more economically conveyed by an impartial body of analysts and administrators—an official or semi-official Consumers' Union in fact. One great argument in favour of this solution is the large saving in resources, both those expended by commerce (much of it in "counter-advertising") and those wasted by the public as a result of unsatisfactory choices.'[11] However, it should be emphasised that, although this proposal may seem fairly sweeping it is definitely in the liberal rather than the radical tradition. Mishan himself justifies it by saying that 'the abolition of commercial advertising cannot seriously be construed as an infringement of libertarian principle'.[12] In contrast, radicals such as Baran and Sweezy argue that commercial advertising is one manifestation of capitalist organisation and as such cannot be treated in isolation from its function on the system as a whole. They contend that policies to control commercial advertising are futile because without the high consumption levels which depend on commercial advertising, monopoly capitalism would face severe depression. More on this in the next chapter.

Failure of the 'Ideal'

The second set of problems relate to the 'ideal' models themselves. The argument here is that, even if it were possible to establish perfect competition, perfect mobility and perfect knowledge, the outcome would not be an efficient allocation of resources. There are three main causes of this.

(a) *Externalities*. External economies and diseconomies of consumption and production have long been recognised as a source of resource misallocation

---

[10] H. G. Johnson, The Economics of Advertising, *The Advertising Quarterly*, No. 13, Autumn 1964, pp. 9-14.
[11] E. J. Mishan, *The Costs of Economic Growth*, Harmondsworth, Penguin Books, 1969, p. 149.
[12] *ibid.*

in market economies. The real issue is whether they are better regarded as peripheral problems or as problems of a central and pervasive nature. Traditionally, liberals have taken the former position but an increasing number now recognise the very general importance of externalities. This is particularly reflected in a growing concern with pollution and congestion. Rothenburg has noted the analytical similarity of these phenomena[13], and mention of them has been made a number of times in earlier chapters, particularly Chapters 4 and 6. They arise primarily because the persons undertaking economic activities which contribute to pollution and congestion are not charged the full social costs of their actions. There are negative 'spillovers' which fall outside the market mechanism. Thus, the private motorist has to meet the cost of petrol and depreciation on his car every time he drives into the city: but he does not normally have to compensate the community for the damage to the environment arising from undertaking that activity. Since no price is attached to the noise and atmospheric pollution he causes, there is a tendency for a higher than optimal level of such activities. Pollution grows and, to the extent that external diseconomies are particularly prevalent in urban areas, so too does congestion, and the two problems compound each other. Similarly, in relation to industrial pollution, Hunt argues that 'the basic economic cause of pollution in a capitalist economy is that business forms do not have to pay for *all* the costs involved in the production process. They pay for labour, raw materials and capital used up in production. But they use the land, air and water for the disposal of waste products that are created in the process of production. Generally, they pay little or nothing for the use of the environment as a garbage disposal.'[14] In these circumstances, environmental destruction is inevitable.

Liberal economists have suggested various potential solutions. These include congestion tolls and effluent taxes, subsidies on activities tending to reduce congestion and pollution, auction by governments of 'rights to pollute', and the use of the legal system as a means of enforcing compensation liability requirements.

However, varied as these policies may first appear, they have much in common. They all are based on the assumption that the fault lies in imperfections in the application of property rights. Thus, the problem with environmental goods, such as clean air and water, is seen to stem from the fact that they are free and hence overused. The unstated assumption is, of course, that the market economy ensures optimal allocation of resources if only all social costs can be internalised. As Edel puts it, 'according to this argument, if a

---

[13] J. Rothenburg, The Economics of Congestion and Pollution: an Integrated View, *The American Economic Review*, Papers and Proceedings, 1970, pp. 114-21.

[14] E. K. Hunt, *Property and Prophets*, New York, Harper and Row, 1972, p. 175.

way could be found to make air and water into property, their owners could rent their use. Competition between those seeking to rent air for smoke disposal and those renting it to breathe, would establish an equilibrium price. The most efficient level of use would result.'[15] However, since air and water are not easily sub-divided (which bit of air are you going to own?), this normally requires the government to establish institutions which put a price on the use of the environment roughly equivalent to that which would result under competitive private ownership.

Of course, there are a tremendous range of problems with regard to public policies of this nature. Which alternative to choose? What level of compensation or tax should be paid by these causing pollution and congestion? In the case of compensation, how should the recipients be identified? How are the damages associated with interdependent activities to be apportioned? These are very considerable practical difficulties and some liberals have suggested that less sophisticated but more easily administered measures of control may be necessary. For example, the provision of 'separate facilities', whereby pollution and congestion are permitted in some areas but prohibited in others, offers a potential way out in at least some cases. But there are many difficulties in this policy too, not the least of which is the influence of income distribution. Since the rich can be expected to inhabit the environmentally attractive areas while the poor are forced by economic circumstances into the less attractive areas, the provision of 'separate facilities' may degenerate into 'economic apartheid'. Of course, this distributional issue is relevant to other environmental control measures as well: in relation to pollution and congestion taxes, for example, one would expect such taxes to be more easily borne by the wealthy sections of the community than by the poor. However, in spite of such problems liberals generally continue to advocate the extended use of the price system as a means of 'environmental fine tuning'. In so doing, they illustrate their ideological association with the principles of the market and of private property rights, and their relative unconcern with income inequality.

(b) *Public Goods.* These are goods and services to which a special kind of external effect applies. The general characteristic is that no price can be charged for them because individuals cannot be barred from sharing the benefits arising from their provision. Hence, they must necessarily be collectively financed. Left to the market economy they will not be provided at all. The responsibility to arrange for their supply has long been recognised as the very

---

[15] M. Edel, *Economies and the Environment*, Englewood Cliffs, New Jersey, Prentice-Hall, 1973, p. 77. Edel's book is generally a good introduction to the analysis of environmental problems and their socio-political roots.

minimum role of Government. The debate nowadays is over the range of such public goods: are they limited to services such as police, 'defence' and street-cleaning, or is the public goods concept more widely applicable to matters such as scientific research, education, health, the arts, and natural resources? Depending on your stance in this debate you either regard public goods as a rather unusual problem with market economies or as a very fundamental one.

Galbraith is one economist who takes the latter view. He has argued most persuasively that the modern American economy is characterised by social imbalance of the sort that requires a major extension of the size of the public sector relative to the private sector.[16] We have had occasion to touch on this important argument before, particularly in Chapters 4 and 6. Suffice it to say here that liberals are not united on the matter, though a survey among American academic economists did indicate 52 per cent in broad agreement with Galbraith (compared with only 13 per cent of businessmen).[17]

(c) *Increasing returns.* Where an increase in output of an industry can be achieved by a less than proportionate increase in the amount of resources used, a situation of increasing returns is said to exist. Under these conditions, perfect competition is an unstable market situation. Thus, as Brownlee and Buttrick note 'it may be that "natural" conditions of production are such that a competitive equilibrium cannot exist e.g. a monopoly may be bound to prevail in some sectors of the economy because of the size of efficient producing units relative to the size of the market'.[18]

Liberals note this problem with regret, because it means that the objectives of productive efficiency and avoidance of large-scale monopolistic organisations cannot be simultaneously achieved. Given this trade-off, some argue that government policy should be introduced to prevent the development of monopoly power, even though this may involve some sacrifice in terms of efficiency. Others argue that the matter should be resolved by nationalisation of the particular industry in question or the introduction of special controls to prevent the abuse of monopoly power. Nationalisation, of course, is generally foreign to liberal ideologists, who see public ownership as an infringement of individual economic freedom. However, it is sometimes rationalised in special circumstances, particularly where the industry is one such as the railways or the provision of electricity or gas, where it is clearly inefficient to have more than one supplier of the service.

[16] See particularly J. K. Galbraith, *The Affluent Society*, Harmondsworth, Penguin Books, 1962, Chapter 18.
[17] C. Hession, *J. K. Galbraith and His Critics,* New York, Mentor, 1972, Appendix.
[18] O. H. Brownlee and J. A. Buttrick, *Producer, Consumer and Social Choice*, New York, McGraw-Hill, 1968, p. 255.

Failure to Achieve Social Objectives

A third set of widely accepted criticisms of market economies concerns their failure to achieve certain social objectives. We examined in Chapter 4 some of the problems involved in identifying community objectives. This is a very complex matter. However, there is fairly widespread agreement on the importance of some specific objectives. Two examples are, (a) reasonable stability of employment and (b) a reasonable degree of equity in the distribution of income and wealth. These objectives are held with varying force by different people and, naturally enough, there are a range of opinions on what is meant by 'reasonable' in both cases. However, practical experience shows how difficult it is to achieve even quite minimal standards. We consider each objective in turn.

It has long been recognised by orthodox economists that market economies are subject to frequent and violent fluctuations. A popular example at the micro level, is the divergent or unstable 'cobweb' model, which illustrates a situation where any disturbance from equilibrium in the market for a particular product will lead to further cumulative movements away from the equilibrium.[19] At the macro level, it is similarly recognised that market economies are commonly characterised by large fluctuations on the aggregate volume of economic activity. Capitalist systems have tended to grow jerkily, with periods of rising prosperity intermixed with periods of depression. Equally importantly, even when in equilibrium, there is no market mechanism ensuring full employment. Particularly since the writings of Keynes it has been recognised that involuntary unemployment is a natural feature of a market economy. (Incidentally, it is interesting to note that it was not until Keynes and in some cases not until long after, that the point gained regular acceptance, though involuntary unemployment had long been empirically observable. Thus, for those classical economists whose models predicted otherwise, there was a clear choice between rejecting the models or rejecting the world: some see it as characteristic that many chose the latter path!) Today it is widely recognised by liberals that government intervention in the economy, largely by controlling aggregate demand through monetary and fiscal policies, is necessary for the stability of employment in capitalist economies.

However, success has been limited. The massive unemployment which characterised the depression years of the 1930's has been avoided, but full employment has been the exception rather than the rule. Hunt and Sherman note that in the United States, 'unemployment for the 1950's and early 1960's averaged 4.6 per cent although it dipped to 3.5 per cent in the mid-1960's'.[20]

[19] See, for example, R. A. Bilas, *Microeconomic Theory*, New York, McGraw-Hill, 1967, pp. 31-33.
[20] E. K. Hunt and H. J. Sherman, *Economics; an Introduction to Traditional and Radical Views*, New York, Harper & Row, 1972, p. 139.

In other countries such as Britain and Australia the average has been much lower, but there have been periodic recessions in which unemployment has been quite significant. Indeed, during the 1970's unemployment has again become a major problem in nearly all developed capitalist economies. The international problem of rapidly accelerating prices has generally caused governments to resort to policies which seek to control inflation by the reduction of aggregate demand. Unemployment has been a quite predictable consequence. Thus, in 1973-4, the percentage of persons registered as unemployed in Great Britain and the United States reached record levels for the post-war period. Even Australia, which has had an unusually good employment record in the post-war period has had to face the problem of significant levels of involuntary unemployment.

Also, it should be noted that national unemployment averages do not reveal the full magnitude of the unemployment problem. Regional variations are important: most countries have problem areas where unemployment problems are particularly severe. Racial and sexual variations are also important: particular social groups are especially vulnerable to problems of unemployment. In the United States, for example, the unemployment rate for blacks has often been over twice that for whites.[21] Taking these points into consideration, we may conclude that, while some progress has been made in respect of full employment objectives, significant problems remain.

Let us now consider the objective of securing a reasonable degree of equity in the distribution of income and wealth. Capitalism as an economic system is based on material incentives and as such some inequality is a necessary condition for its continued operation. Nevertheless, governments in most capitalist countries apparently seek to reduce the degree of inequality which would naturally result from the workings of the market. Economists of liberal persuasion have generally supported such moves for reform, and have lent support to the belief that government redistributive policies are likely to be effective. Thus Leftwich asserts that 'redistribution of resources can be accomplished within the framework of the price system and the free enterprise economy'.[22] There is certainly a wide range of available policy instruments. The most important are as follows:

(1) minimum wage legislation;
(2) progressive income taxation and capital gains taxation;
(3) redistribution of labour resources through education, retraining schemes, etc.;

---

[21] For information on the racial dimension of the unemployment problem see P. Baran and P. Sweezy, *Monopoly Capital*, Harmondsworth, Penguin Books, 1968, Chapter 9, or D. M. Gordon, *Problems in Political Economy: An Urban Perspective*, New York, D. C. Heath, 1971, Chapter 2.

[22] R. H. Leftwich, *The Price System and Resource Allocation*, Fourth Edition, Hinsdale, Illinois, The Dryden Press, 1970, pp. 355-366.

(4) redistribution of capital resources through wealth taxes and estate duties.

However, each is subject to important limitations as a means of securing greater equity in the distribution of income. Most studies of the effect of income taxation, for example, show that in practice it is not progressive at all; tax normally accounts for a similar (and sometimes higher) proportion of poor people's income than of rich people's income.[23] The overall impact of government redistributive policies on the extremes of income and poverty is generally rather marginal. Thus, in the United States in 1970 (after many years of effort by the government to tackle the poverty problem) 25.5 millions lived in families with an annual income of less than $3,900, the officially designated 'poverty level'. On the other hand the wealthiest 5 per cent of the American population received over 20 per cent of all income, and within this latter group a number had an average income per *hour* in excess of $3,900![24] The reader is left to judge whether this constitutes reasonable equity in the distribution of income and wealth.

Problems of the Liberal Stance

Many of the public policies described in this chapter are subject to specific problems. Some policies such as pollution and congestion taxes may improve allocative efficiency only at the expense of other objectives such as a reasonable degree of income equality. Others, such as policies to establish 'workable competition' may have adverse effects on the level of production costs, especially in industries characterised by increasing returns. Moreover, there is always the problem of knowing how far public policy should go: should the Government restrict itself to 'fine tuning' or should it seek to extend the public sector significantly so as to redress what Galbraith calls the 'social imbalance' between the public and private sectors. Then, whichever way this sort of issue is resolved, there is always the problem of choosing the best policy instruments.

This chapter ends by considering three more fundamental problems of the liberal stance. The first is a fairly technical point, but one with important

---

[23] See, for example, G. Kolko, Taxation and Inequality, in D. M. Gordon, *Problems in Political Economy: An Urban Perspective*, New York, D. C. Heath, 1971 and B. L. Embury & N. Podder, Economic Welfare in Australia, in P. R. Wilson (Ed.) *Australian Social Issues of the 70's*, Sydney, Butterworths, 1972, and B. A. Musgrave, Estimating the Distribution of the Tax Burden, in *Income and Wealth*, Series 10, Cambridge, Bowes and Bowes, 1964.

[24] See D. Mermelstein (Ed.), *Economics: Mainstream Readings and Radical Critiques*, New York, Random House, 1970, part 3A and R. C. Edwards, M. Reich and T. E. Weisskopf, (Eds.) *The Capitalist System*, Englewood Cliffs, New Jersey, 1972. Chapter 5.

implications. The other two are of a more explicitly radical nature, and thereby serve to provide a link with the following chapter.

(a) *The theory of the second best.* One of the most important theorems in microeconomic theory is that developed by Lipsey and Lancaster known as the theory of the second best.[25] In brief this theorem states, on the basis of a mathematical argument, that, in a situation characterised by *any* deviation from a social optimum, policy measures which eliminate only some of the departures from the optimum may well result in a net decrease in social welfare. Thus, even if a general optimum can be identified, a move towards it is not necessarily better than a move away, if the optimum itself cannot be achieved in practice. Intuitively, most students understand this: in relation to examinations, for example, we might be agreed that the optimum situation would be to have no examinations, but that, if this ideal is not attainable (due to reactionary university administrators perhaps), then it might be more desirable to have a larger rather than smaller number of examinations. Similarly, in relation to industrial structure, if perfect competition is not attainable in all markets, then it may not be desirable to seek to establish it in some of them.

The implications of this for the liberal attitude to public policy are quite important. *Ad hoc* policies aimed at the partial fulfillment of the conditions for competitive equilibrium may result in effects diametrically opposed to those desired. Now it may be true, as Mishan[26] notes, that in certain circumstances (for example, where markets are fairly clearly segmented) second-best problems may be unimportant. However, the general rationale for the liberal approach to public policy is considerably undermined.

(b) *The concept of popular sovereignty.* Many radical economists pick on this concept as the central flaw in the liberal argument. Sweezy described the problem as follows: 'There is a tendency on the part of modern liberal theorists to interpret the state as an institution established in the interests of society as a whole for the purpose of mediating and reconciling the antagonisms to which social existence inevitably gives rise . . . (However) the class-mediation theory assumes, usually implicitly, that the underlying class structure, or what comes to the same thing, the system of property relations is an immutable datum, in this respect like the order of nature itself . . . (but) the superficiality of this assumption is indicated by the most cursory study of history. The fact is that many forms of property relations with their concomitant

[25] R. G. Lipsey & K. Lancaster, The General Theory of Second Best, *The Review of Economic Studies*, Vol. XXIII, 1956-7, pp. 11-32.

[26] E. J. Mishan, Second Thoughts on Second Best, *Oxford Economic Papers*, October 1962, pp. 205-217.

class structures have come and gone in the past, and there is no reason to assume that they will not continue to do so in the future. The class structure of society is no part of the natural order of things; it is the product of past social development, and it will change in the course of future social development. Once this is recognized it becomes clear that the liberal theory goes wrong in the manner in which it initially poses the problem. We cannot ask: given a certain class structure, how will the various classes, with their divergent and often conflicting interests, manage to get along together? We must ask: how did a particular class structure come into being and by what means is its continued existence guaranteed? As soon as an attempt is made to answer this question, it appears that the state has a function in society which is prior to and more fundamental than any which present-day liberals attribute to it.'[27]

The inadequacy of the popular sovereignty view of government capitalist society is widely recognised by political scientists. Members of government act at least partially in terms of self-interest. Further, to the extent that the government constitutes a political elite, and to the extent that the political elite has shared or overlapping interests with other elites, then the government can be seen as embodying class interests. If this point is accepted, then we can hardly rely on the government as an institution to correct the whole range of problems arising from the market economy. We can only rely on it to introduce such reforms as are consistent with a particular class interest.

(c) *The interconnectedness of economic problems.* Radicals further argue that the liberal attitude to the various economic problems of the market economy is too superficial. They argue that, far from being a matter for piecemeal analysis, the problems are interconnected. They have a common source in the capitalist system of economic organisation, with its fundamental principles of private property ownership and exchange through the market. Together with the radicals' further argument for a broader approach to the appraisal of economic systems, this proposition provides the central focus of the next chapter.

[27] P. Sweezy, *The Theory of Capitalist Development*, New York, Monthly Review Press, 1942, pp. 240-242.

CHAPTER EIGHT

Radical Alternatives

Neo-classical economics and the associated approach to public policy have recently been the subject of intensive criticism. The list of prominent dissenters grows annually. For example, the distinguished British economist Nicholas Kaldor has come out as a strong critic of economic orthodoxy; he contends that 'the powerful attraction of the habits of thought engendered by "equilibrium economics" has become a major obstacle to the development of economics as a science'.[1] The introduction to a book by economist Robert Heilbroner begins by raising the 'disturbing question of whether economic theory, as it is presently constituted, is in fact a useful instrument to achieve desired social ends of any kind whatever'.[2] Galbraith has argued that orthodox economics has degenerated to the status of a 'supporting faith', recalling Marx's description of economists as 'the scientific representatives of the bourgeoisie'. In his presidential address to the American Economic Association he (Galbraith not Marx!) further argues that 'for a new and notably articulate generation of economists a reference to neo-classical economics has, become markedly pejorative. I would judge as well as hope that the present attack will be decisive.'[3]

The most common accusation against neo-classical theory is that it has become increasingly sophisticated only at the expense of becoming decreasingly relevant. It is argued that it provides a very constricting framework in which to study the operations of the capitalist society. The emphasis on problems of resource allocation and the neglect of broader issues such as equity, environmental quality, and resource creation is particularly subject to criticism.

Some radicals argue that neo-classical theory is worse than irrelevant, that it is systematically misleading. Because it diverts attention away from the real workings of the economic system and the problems it creates, it performs

---

[1] N. Kaldor, The Irrelevance of Equilibrium Economics, *The Economic Journal*, Dec. 1972, pp. 1237-1255.

[2] R. L. Heilbroner, *Economic Means and Social Ends*, Englewood Cliffs, N.J. Prentice-Hall, 1969, p. VII.

[3] J. K. Galbraith, Power and the Useful Economist, *The American Economic Review*, March, 1973, p. 1.

an ideological function. Ideologies in social science are systems of ideas which provide a moral justification for a particular type of socio-economic system. Radicals argue that orthodox economics contains strong ideological elements, in that it provides an apparent legitimacy for the capitalist system. Even Lipsey, whose own textbook is far from radical, agrees that, 'even the best American textbooks manage to convey the idea that economic theory justifies the private-enterprise market economies found in most Western countries'.[4]

Radicals see a link between problems of neo-classical economics and of capitalist systems in practice. Since neo-classical economics performs an ideological role, it systematically emphasises the most favourable aspects of the capitalist system and neglects the problematic areas. Hence, the rejection of the neo-classical framework and the direct study of the problems of capitalism typically go hand in hand. This chapter looks at some of the dimensions which radicals seek to introduce into their analysis so as to bring more sharply into focus the functioning of capitalist systems.

First, we need to be clear about the delineation of radical economics. This is important because the term is often loosely used. Three groups of modern economists are sometimes described as radical:

(a) *Marxists and neo-Marxists.* The greatest of all critics of capitalism was Karl Marx, and his ideas continue to provide a great inspiration for significant numbers of economists. A distinction is sometimes drawn between Marxists and neo-Marxists, according to the extent to which their analysis has 'revisionist' elements. However, there is broad agreement on the main problems to be tackled (for example, class conflict, exploitation and imperialism) and the methodology to be applied. Also, there is general agreement regarding the necessity of revolutionary change. Some of the most prominent members of this school include Paul Sweezy, Maurice Dobb, Harry Magdoff, Ernest Mandel and the late Paul Baran.

The number of Marxists in universities is comparatively small, partly because of victimisation of scholars with such dangerous views.[5] However, there has been a recent intensification of interest among younger economists reflected, among other things, in the formation in the United States of a Union of Political Economists which publishes a Marxist-oriented journal called the *Review of Radical Political Economics.*

---

[4] R. G. Lipsey, *An Introduction to Positive Economics*, London, Weidenfeld and Nicholson, London, 1967, p. XIV.

[5] For illustration of this point see L. S. Lifschultz, Could Karl Marx Teach Economics in America, *Ramparts.* April, 1974, pp. 27-60.

(b) *Institutionalists and Neo-Institutionalists.* This second group of economists share certain commitments with the Marxists (a rejection of the static methodology of neo-classical economics, a realisation of the need for critical analysis and for such analysis to be developed in terms of the particular historical characteristics of individual countries). However, there are important differences, such as the attitude to theory *per se* and to the possibility of significant social change through reform rather than through revolution. Institutionalists usually put strong emphasis on the descriptive rather than the deductive approach to economic analysis, and usually (though not invariably) take a reformist stance in relation to public policy questions. The 'founding father' of institutionalist economics was Thorstein Veblen, and the tradition was carried on (mainly in America) by Mitchell, Commons, Means and others. The best known modern representatives are J. K. Galbraith and Gunnar Myrdal. As a whole, the group is less cohesive than the Marxists, though there is an American organisation called The Association for Evolutionary Economics which was formed in 1958 to provide some focus for economists of this particular persuasion.[6]

(c) *Neo-classicists with a social conscience.* Concern with problems such as racial and sexual discrimination, poverty, congestion and pollution sometimes appears to be sufficient basis for an economist to be classified as radical. E. J. Mishan, to whose work reference has been made many times in the book, is an obvious example. However, it should be recognised that the methodology used tends to be supportive of conservative conclusions. This certainly tends to be the case when neo-classical economic methodology is applied to the study of social problems. Mishan's book on *The Costs of Economic Growth* has large elements of 'good old days' conservatism in it. The work of American economist Gary Becker provides an even better illustration: he has applied orthodox analysis to the study of discrimination, household time allocations, education and a number of other social issues but his conclusions are generally supportive of the *status quo.* Racial discrimination, for example, is described as arising because association with Negroes has a disutility to whites, and neo-classical tools are adopted to show how such discrimination, far from being accentuated by capitalism, actually tends to reduce the profits of capitalist employers. As far as the model is concerned the origins of the disutility are not important. While applauding their willingness to deal with matters often regarded as 'not strictly economic', it must be recognised that economists

---

[6] For a discussion of the significance of institutionalist economics and the work of some of the most prominent institutionalist economists, see A. G. Gruchy, *Contemporary Economic Thought,* London, Macmillan, 1972.

like Becker are very far from radical in terms of the political dimensions of their analysis.[7]

Like any classification, this one is not without its problems. Some prominent critics of conventional economics, such as Boulding and Heilbroner, are not so easily categorised. Nevertheless, as a primary classification it is useful, mainly because it distinguishes Marxists from other non-conformist groups on the grounds of their analytical structure and ideological commitment. It saves much confusion if the term radical is reserved for the Marxists and neo-Marxists. The other two groups typically emphasise the need for—and potential success of—reformist policies within the capitalist system. Economists in the Marxian tradition reject this. They argue that the analysis of the capitalist system leads to a recognition of the need for (and inevitability of) revolutionary change.

The remainder of this chapter is in the Marxian tradition, although some of the points made are 'revisionist' in the sense that they are concerned with the up-dating and modification of Marxian arguments in the light of twentieth-century developments in the capitalist economy. The main theme is that there is a need to analyse and appraise the capitalist system in a broader framework than that provided by orthodox economics. Thus, the structure of the chapter is determined by the major dimensions which radicals seek to introduce into the analysis. These include:

(1)   the dynamics of social change;
(2)   class conflict;
(3)   imperialism and militarism;
(4)   the role of the state;
(5)   the relationship between the economic base and social superstructure of capitalism.

The Dynamics of Social Change

Firstly radicals argue that there is a need to introduce a historical dimension into the appraisal of economic systems. Among other things, this serves to emphasise the potential impermanence of capitalism (or of any other economic system) and the process by which socio-economic systems are transformed. Thus, Hunt and Schwartz argue that a major objection to orthodox economics is its 'total lack of historical perspective—capitalism is accepted as for all time—its past evolution from feudalism is dealt with summarily, other systems are discussed only to underline the superiority of capitalism'.[8] It is true that

---

[7]   See G. S. Becker, *The Economics of Discrimination,* Chicago, University of Chicago Press, 1957.
[8]   E. K. Hunt and J. G. Schwartz, (Eds.) *A Critique of Economic Theory*, Harmondsworth, Penguin Books, 1972, p. 8.

this criticism is not valid when applied to the work of many economic historians but the very separation of economics from economic history makes it possible for economists to ignore the potential impermanence of the systems they study. Of course, this is of central importance to Marxists who argue that the structure of society is neither God-given nor rooted in the laws of nature.

Marx argued that social systems are subject to dramatic change and that they change because of internal contradictions inherent in them, rather than because of the rationality and humanity of mankind. Social change thereby arises from conflict rather than consensus. This is usually specified as a dialectical process, a process of thesis, antithesis and synthesis. In relation to the capitalist system, the internal contradictions are seen as producing a growing antithesis in terms of class conflict; such conflict has revolutionary potential which eventually becomes unleashed and transforms the whole social order. Capitalism is thereby replaced by socialism.

Radicals often do not adhere tightly to the dialectical view of social change. Rather, as Ward notes, to describe society as being in a state of dialectic tension is usually taken to mean two things, 'first, that the balance of forces is not stable, so that relatively small changes in the environment may precipitate large change in social states: second, that the situation is open-ended in the sense that any of a number of factors may be the precipitant of the next round of changes'.[9] Whether one adopts the strict Marxian view of the dialectic or this looser approach, conflict and instability are the focus of attention. This, of course, is in stark contrast with economists in the neo-classical tradition who, as we have seen throughout this book, adopt an analytical approach which emphasises harmony of interests, tendencies towards equilibrium and non-disruptive change.[10] Naturally, this difference of view manifests itself in different attitudes to social change: whereas neo-classicists concern themselves with 'fine-tuning' allocation problems, radicals concentrate on an analysis of the revolutionary forces within the society.

The Class Structure of Capitalism

The second dimension of radical analysis centres on the concept of social class. This follows on from the previous point in that class is seen as the

[9] B. Ward, *What's Wrong With Economics*, London, Macmillan, 1972, p. 63.

[10] The role of conservative ideology in determining this orientation of neo-classical theory is well expressed by Joan Robinson: 'The dominance of equilibrium was excused by the fact that it is excessively complicated to bring into a single model both movements of the whole through time and the detailed interaction of the parts. It was necessary for purely intellectual reasons to choose between a simple dynamic model and an elaborate static one. But it was no accident that the static one was chosen; the soothing harmonies of equilibrium supported *laissez-faire* ideology and the elaboration of the argument kept us all too busy to have any time for dangerous thoughts', *Economic Philosophy*, Harmondsworth, Penguin Books, 1962, p. 70.

focus of conflict in capitalist society and it is antagonism between classes which eventually leads to the destruction of the system. Marxists argue that class conflict has been a central feature of all previous forms of social organisation, such as slave and feudal systems: 'the history of all hitherto existing society is the history of class struggles'.[11]

The original Marxian conception is quite simple. Capitalist society is seen as being stratified into two main groups, those who derive their income principally from the ownership of capital resources—the bourgeoisie—and those who derive their income principally from hiring out their labour resources—the proletariat. This economically-based class structure is seen as the fundamental feature of capitalist organisation. It provides the basis for systematic exploitation of one class by the other. Such exploitation arises because labour is not paid the full value of what it produces. Marx followed in the tradition of Ricardo, in believing the value of a commodity to be determined by the amount of labour time necessary for its production. Surplus value is then seen as arising because capitalists buy one commodity—labour—and sell another— that which labour produces in the production process. Profits exist because the value of commodities sold exceed the cost of the labour employed, all other factors having been reduced to embodied labour-time. Since labour is the only source of value, profits cannot be justified, as the neo-classists typically seek to justify them, as the return for an input such as managerial ability or as a return for risk-taking. In the Marxian framework they must be seen as a surplus payment, a 'rip-off', indicating exploitation by one social class or another.

What happens to the profits? Of course, the bourgeoisie can be expected to use some part in consumption activities, but a proportion will normally be ploughed back in order to increase capital and hence future profits. Indeed, further accumulation of capital is normally seen by Marxists as an inevitable consequence of competition between capitalists. Since profit-motivated firms can be expected to be constantly developing new methods of production, no single firm can be stationary. In Marx's words, 'the development of capitalist production makes it constantly necessary to keep increasing the amount of capital laid out in a given industrial undertaking, and competition makes the immanent laws of capitalist production to be felt by each individual capitalist as external coercive laws. It compels him to keep constantly expanding his capital, in order to preserve it, but extend it he cannot except by means of progressive accumulation.'[12] Therefore, the capitalist system can be expected to be characterised by concentration of economic activity in the hands

---

[11] K. Marx and F. Engels, *Manifesto of the Communist Party*, Moscow, Foreign Languages Publishing House, p. 45.

[12] K. Marx, *Capital*, Volume 1, Moscow, Foreign Languages Publishing House, 1961, p. 592.

of larger and larger firms. This in turn further increases the scope for exploitation of the working class.

Of course, it is extremely important to question the appropriateness of the Marxian analysis of class and exploitation in the light of developments in the social structure of capitalist economies. Many sociologists, for example, have argued that a more sophisticated theory is needed to explain the observed pattern of social stratification. Max Weber, for example, suggested that dimension of social status and power must be considered in addition to class since these elements of social stratification need not necessarily coincide. More recently, others have taken the position that social stratification is so complex that a multi-dimensional approach is needed, social groups being defined in terms of a whole range of variables such as status, sex, age and race as well as economically-based class. Others recognise these dimensions but argue that the class division remains the best starting point for social analysis. Parkin is a good example of the latter group: he argues that the two class model is still useful but redefines the classes in terms of the white collar: blue collar dichotomy.[13]

Radicals typically seek to retain the essence of the original Marxian conception. Of course, Marx himself was not as crude in this respect as is sometimes implied, recognising the existence of intermediate social groups such as the petit bourgeoisie (typically the self-employed shopkeeper or tradesman). Also, Marxists have always recognised the problem of 'false consciousness', whereby social attitudes and aspirations are out of line with class position as determined by a person's relationship to the means of production. It is important to remember that class is determined by economic position (ownership of resources). This helps in appraising the significance of the growth of the so-called white-collar 'middle class'. The prime source of the income of this group is the sale of their labour, so their relationship to the means of production is generally that of the proletariat. Their tendency to have bourgeois aspirations and views which undermine the revolutionary potential of capitalist society is not indicative of their class position so much as their false-consciousness.

A second difficulty with the Marxian view of social class is sometimes said to arise from the change in the nature of business conduct. As a result of the so-called 'managerial revolution', whereby ownership of the large corporation has become separated from control, it is held that the exploitive mode of behaviour typically associated with capitalist enterprise has all but disappeared. Thus, the chairman of a major United States company asserted some years ago

---

[13] F. Parkin, *Class, Inequality and Political Order,* London, Paladin, 1972, Parkin's book is a useful introduction to various aspects of social stratification.

that 'the historic complaint that big business, as the producing arm of capitalism, exploited the many for the profit of the few and deprived the workers of the product of their own labour had a valid basis in the facts of European capitalism, but lacks substance when applied to American capitalism today'.[14] One economist has gone so far as to describe the typical large modern firm as 'a soulful corporation'.[15]

Various social scientists have sought to handle this phenomenon in different ways. Galbraith identifies one particular group within the firm which he calls the technostructure. This group embraces 'all who bring specialised knowledge, talent or experience to group decision making'.[16] Since this is where corporate power is seen to lie, Galbraith implies that the traditional function and identity of the bourgeoisie are no longer. The technostructure is not bourgeois in terms of its class position: its members are salaried and, Galbraith argues, they can be expected to base decisions on criteria somewhat different to the more traditional owner-managers. Andreas Papandreau disagrees. While recognising the technostructure as the group with apparent control over resources, he regards it as the servant of the bourgeoisie: a group of labour which is internally divided according to specialised skills and which lacks power as a social class. In his own words, 'they (the members of the technostructure), become tamed and assimilated into the corporate Establishment, not as a new guiding force, but as a tool of the managerial elite'.[17]

It is this last view which is the most widely held among radicals. They argue that some superficial features of business enterprise may have changed as a result of the 'managerial revolution' but the function of firms within the economic system has not. Salaried managers may like to argue that they are guided by a feeling of social responsibility and, indeed, benevolence in their business decisions. However, this is mainly to rationalise and legitimise their role as instruments of the propertied class. When the pursuit of benevolent behaviour is in conflict with profitability it is invariably terminated. Furthermore, the high incidence of criminal activities by big corporations hardly suggests 'soulful' behaviour. It would seem appropriate to conclude that there is little reason to doubt that the quest for profits is as pronounced among managers as among 'owner-capitalists': the changes in the means by which private enterprise proceeds constitute an institutionalisation of the capitalist function rather than a disappearance of it.

[14] Quoted in R. L. Heilbroner, *The Limits of American Capitalism*, New York, Harper and Row, 1966, pp. 31-2.
[15] C. Kaysen, The Social Significance of the Modern Corporation, *The American Economic Review*, May 1957, p. 314.
[16] J. K. Galbraith, *The New Industrial State*, Harmondsworth, Penguin Books, p. 80.
[17] A. G. Papandreau, *Paternalistic Capitalism*, Minneapolis, University of Minnesota Press, 1972, p. 73.

A third problem sometimes raised to demonstrate the inappropriateness of the Marxian model concerns the diffusion of capital ownership. It is argued that ownership of capital has become so widespread that it is no longer possible to identify a capitalist class. As one commentator has put it, 'The economy of the United States is rapidly assuming the character of what may be termed "People's Capitalism", under which the production facilities of the nation—notably manufacturing—have come to be increasingly owned by people in the middle and lower income brackets or indirectly by mutual institutions which manage their savings'.[18] The argument has *some* power. In particular, if it were true that shareholdings were becoming more widespread and that such shareholdings could be used to control corporate behaviour, then the 'people's capitalism' argument would have some credibility. But most of the evidence suggests otherwise. Perlo, for example, notes that in the United States the percentage of population owning stocks has fallen since 1930. He concludes that 'the basic claim of "people's capitalism", that the rank and file of the population are becoming owners of the means of production in American industry, is without basis in fact'.[19] There is no doubt that the great bulk of property is still held in very few hands. Official American figures reveal that in 1966, 1 per cent of all taxpayers received 74 per cent of total dividends and 1 per cent received 76 per cent of all capital gains.[20] It is by pointing to figures such as these that radicals reject the argument that diffusion of ownership has broken down the class conflict. Moreover, they note that, even though members of the proletariat may own shares, the proportion of total shareholdings of each corporation is typically minute, and the diffusion of the shareholders is such as to obviate any possibility of small shareholders exercising command over resources. Certainly, such small shareholdings do not invalidate the basic proposition of the radical view, that the interests of the two principal social classes are in fundamental conflict.

Imperialism and Militarism

The conflicts arising from capitalism also have an international dimension. The behaviour of individual capitalists is typically aggressively expansive; applied in the international sphere, this is seen as giving rise to the inter-related phenomena of imperialism and militarism. People of all political

---

[18] Marcus Nedler, quoted in V. Perlo, 'People's Capitalism' and Stock Ownership, *The American Economic Review*, Volume 48, No. 3, June 1958, pp. 333-347.

[19] V. Perlo, 'People's Capitalism' and Stock Ownership, *The American Economic Review*, Volume 48, No. 3, June 1958, p. 343.

[20] Information on the distribution of wealth and income from capital is to be found in R. J. Lampman, *The Share of Top Wealth-Holders in National Wealth*, 1922-1956, National Bureau of Economic Research, New Jersey, Princeton University Press, 1962, and F. Lundberg, *The Rich and the Super-Rich,* New York, Lyle Stuart Inc., 1968.

persuasions often express sorrow for the plight of the underdeveloped world and concern that there is little sign of narrowing in the prosperity gap between the rich and poor nations. Similarly, people of all political persuasions frequently have an abhorrence of warfare and regret that it appears necessary to engage in high levels of military expenditure. Radicals contend that these problems are inherent in capitalist organisation.

Sweezy defines the characteristics of imperialism as a stage in the development of the world economy in which '(a) several advanced capitalist countries stand on a competitive footing with respect to the world market for industrial products; (b) monopoly capital is the dominant form of capital; and (c) the contradictions of the accumulation process have reached such maturity that capital export is an outstanding feature of world economic relations. As a consequence of these basic economic conditions, we have two further characteristics: (d) severe rivalry in the world market leading alternately to cutthroat competition and international monopoly combines; and (c) the territorial division of "unoccupied" parts of the world among the major capitalist powers (and their satellites).'[21]

The analysis of imperialism is quite well developed; the works of Lenin, Hobson and Rosa Luxemburg provided a basis on which more recent works by Baran, Frank, Magdoff and others have built.[22] The unifying theme of these writings is the emphasis on the asymmetry of development in the expoiting and exploited nations: the prosperity of the former and the poverty of the latter are two sides of the same coin. The following passage from the Belgian Marxist Ernest Mandel summarises the argument: 'Born in Western Europe, industrial capitalism spread in the course of a century over the entire world. But this expansion assumed a very special form: all the countries in the world became outlets, sources of raw material and, to a smaller extent, fields of investment for capital. But the capitalist mode of production, and in particular the large capitalist factory, touched only the periphery of the economic life of these continents. This is, briefly, the cause of the phenomenon which is today known, shamefacedly, by the euphemism of "underdevelopment". . . . The economic under-development of the colonial and semi-colonial countries is a result of imperialist penetration and domination, and is maintained, preserved and intensified by this domination. To eliminate it is the fundamental condition for clearing the way to progress; it is even more

---

[21] P. Sweezy, *The Theory of Capitalist Development*, London, Dobson, 1949, p. 307.

[22] See, for example, P. Baran, *The Political Economy of Growth*, New York, Monthly Review Press, 1962, A. G. Frank, *Capitalism and Underdevelopment in Latin America*, New York, Monthly Review Press, 1968, and H. Magdoff, *The Age of Imperialism*, New York, Monthly Review Press, 1969.

important than the removal of the native ruling classes, though the two processes are usually inter-connected.'[23]

The main reasons for the continued subordination of the poor to the rich
countries can be classified as follows:

(a) *The demonstration effect.* Consumption patterns in the rich countries
are emulated by those in the poor countries which tends to make them oriented
towards characteristically foreign types of goods.

(b) *The monopoly effect.* Large foreign firms typically have great advantages with respect to finance, technology, and so on, and tend to dominate
domestic enterprise. This is particularly accentuated by the dominance of
the giant multinational corporations. Their economic power is immense:
the revenues of individual firms are often many times the gross national
product of individual underdeveloped countries. By determining their sphere
of operation according to where the profit potential is highest, without regard
to the needs and aspirations of the countries in which they operate, they tend
to destroy local initiatives and entrepreneurial activity.

(c) *The brain-drain effect.* Though small in absolute size, the emigration
of educated professionals from the poor to the rich countries, has a major
effect in terms of depleting the human resources of the poor nations.

(d) *The factor-bias effect.* The production techniques employed in the poor
countries are often influenced by techniques used in the rich countries and
are usually more capital-intensive than is desirable from the viewpoint of the
labour-abundant poor countries.[24]

The internationalisation of capital also has important political dimensions
which add to the problem of underdevelopment. In part, such political functions are carried out by firms themselves. For example, there may be alliances
between foreign corporations and the domestic bourgeoisie designed to give
political protection against potential internal challenge. As Baran has argued,
'Small wonder that under such circumstances Western big business heavily en-
gaged in raw materials exploitation leaves no stone unturned to obstruct the
evolution of social and political conditions in under-developed countries that
might be conducive to their economic development. It uses its tremendous
power to prop up the backward areas' comprador administrations, to disrupt
and corrupt the social and political movements that oppose them, and to overthrow whatever progressive governments may rise to power and refuse to do the

[23] E. Mandel, *Marxist Economic Theory*, London, Merlin Press, 1968, pp. 441 and 476.
[24] This classification is adapted from T. E. Weisskopf, Underdevelopment and the Future of
the Poor Countries, *The Review of Radical Political Economy*, Spring 1972, p. 9-11.

bidding of their imperialistic overlords.'[25] More generally, the political auto-
nomy of the poor countries is limited by their dependent position. So long as
the poor countries seek aid from the advanced capitalist countries and the
international organisations mainly funded by them, nationalistic political
tendencies must usually be curtailed.

The governments of the imperialist nations play a further role. As Sweezy
notes, 'monopoly capital needs to expand abroad, and for this purpose it
requires the assistance and protection of the state. It is, therefore, here that
we find the roots of imperialist policy with its manifold implications.'[26] It is
in this connection that militarism is so important. International warfare is at
least partly explicable in terms of the desire to expand or maintain markets.
Marxists argue that the great wars of redivision of the twentieth century can
interpreted as economically-based conflicts between rival capitalist powers.
More recent military intervention in Vietnam and Cambodia can be similarly
interpreted as attempts by American capitalism (with Australian and New
Zealand support) to maintain market position in the 'third world'.

Militarism is also necessary to maintain stability in the imperialist nations'
own economies. Thus, Baran and Sweezy explain the high levels of American
military expenditure as part of the attempt to absorb the productive surplus
of that nation.[27] They argue that productive capacity has outstripped the
level of 'socially necessary production'. As such, ways must be found of dis-
posing of the surplus, or otherwise the economy would be plunged into depression. One method of surplus disposal is associated with 'the sales effort',
an attempt to persuade consumers to raise their consumption demands by
convincing them through advertising that they need commodities which they previously did not realise they needed! Another method of surplus disposal is
military expenditure. Indeed, this is the most 'ideal' method of all: the surplus
productive resources can be used in producing bombs, fighter 'planes and tanks
which can then be stockpiled. The problem is that, while these goods (can this
term be applied here without normative association?) are not marketed in
consumers' markets, a demand for them must necessarily be created—a political demand. It becomes necessary for the government to justify the high
levels of military expenditure, typically through arguments of the 'protection
from communist aggression' nature. Also, it seems necessary to explode the
bombs in other countries from time to time for, while this is not necessary
for surplus absorption (the bombs only need be stockpiled), it is necessary for
maintaining the credibility of the military expenditure programme. Radicals

[25] P. Baran, *The Political Economy of Growth*, New York, Monthly Review Press, 1969, p. 198.
[26] P. Sweezy, *The Theory of Capitalism and Underdevelopment in Latin America*, New York, Monthly Review Press, 1968, p. 314-5.
[27] P. Baran and P. Sweezy, *Monopoly Capital*, Harmondsworth, Penguin Books, 1968.

typically see this as the ultimate irrationality of the capitalist system: that, in order to maintain itself, it must allocate resources to socially destructive ends.

The State in Capitalist Society

This brings us to a more general consideration of the role of the State in capitalist society. It is a characteristic of radical analysis that the State is subject to analysis. This is in contrast with the more orthodox view of neoclassical economists who (to the extent that they bother at all) base their analysis of the State on the implicit assumption of popular sovereignty. In O'Connor's words, 'The traditional school . . . describes individual needs and desires as they are transfigured by a voting process into State economic activity. The State economy is reduced to the totality of personal needs.'[28] But this simply will not do for the radicals. To them, the view of the State as the embodiment of community rather than class interests is quite unacceptable.

The radical view of the State is described by Paul Sweezy as a 'class-domination theory' as distinct from a 'class-mediation theory'.[29] The class structure of society is based on a set of property relations and the property owning classes are thereby distinguished from the owned and non-owning. But the stability of the system requires a special institution to protect those property relations. This is the primary function of the State. By the use of force—either through the legal system or more directly through police intimidation and brutality—the interests of one class are protected from the challenges of the other. The forms by which the State maintains the stability of the social order are many and varied and a useful distinction is sometimes drawn between the 'repressive State apparatus' and the 'ideological State apparatus'.

The legal system in capitalist societies is an example of the first aspect in that it helps to protect the vested interests of the bourgeoisie. Of course, the function of any legal system is necessarily conservative in that it serves to stabilise the existing structure of society. However, this is sometimes said to have particularly odious consequences under capitalism in that offences against property are often more heavily punished than offences against people, reflecting an economic substructure in which property is the more highly valued. So, while the legal system does provide the opportunity in some cases for the lower classes to take action against the upper, its general function is socially repressive.

[28] J. O'Connor, Scientific and Ideological Elements in the Economic Theory of Government Policy, *Science and Society*, 1969, pp. 385-414, reprinted in E. K. Hunt and J. G. Schwartz (Eds.) *A Critique of Economic Theory*, Harmondsworth, Penguin Books, 1972, pp. 367-396.

[29] P. Sweezy, *The Theory of Capitalist Development*, London, Dobson, 1949, p. 243.

Ideological means by which social stability is maintained include all forms of dissemination of ideas and information which reduce the challenge to the existing social order. Any social system will be characterised by a dominant ideology which provides it with some sort of legitimacy. The usual pro-Establishment bias of the media provides an obvious example. The dominance of neo-classical theory in economics courses may be regarded as another. Similarly, the Church is another long-established target of radical criticism because it disseminates an ideology which contributes to the 'false-consciousness' of the working class ('we'll all be equal in the after-life so there is no need to worry about inequality in this one'). Such ideologies serve to defuse potential political radicalism. It should be emphasised that ideologies seldom have universal acceptance; the important question is 'which ideologies are dominant?' It is by supporting ruling-class ideologies against other contenders that the State plays a stabilising role.

A further function of the State is to prevent inter-capitalist rivalries. Hunt expresses the point as follows: 'Each capitalist is interested only in his own profits, and therefore, it is inevitable that the interests of capitalists will clash. If not resolved, many of these clashes would threaten the very existence of the system. Thus, the government intervenes, and in doing so, it protects the viability of the capitalist system. This is why it is sometimes possible to observe the government acting in a way that is contrary to the interests of some of the capitalists. But the government never acts in a way that is contrary to the interest of all capitalists, taken as a class.'[30] Again, the State is seen as a socially stabilising force which acts in a systematically class-biased manner.

We may conclude that for those committed to improvement of the relative position of the non-property-owning classes, the State is part of the problem. Of course, it is true that concessions can be wrought by the working class through the use of political channels. The achievement of a shorter working week is one obvious example. These concessions may markedly improve the absolute well-being of the non-property-owners. However, the concesssions are granted largely so that challenge to the existing political and economic order will be minimised. Thus, the State apparatus is more a mechanism for the maintenance of stability than for the initiation of radical change. Sweezy sums up the radical position as follows: 'In the first place, the State comes into action in the economic sphere in order to solve problems which are posed by the development of capitalism. In the second place, where the interests of the capitalist class are concerned, there is a strong predisposition to use the State power freely. And, finally, the State may be used to make concessions to the working class

---

[30] E. K. Hunt, *Property and Prophets*, New York, Harper & Row, 1972, p. 87.

provided that the consequences of not doing so are sufficiently dangerous to the stability and functioning of the system as a whole.'[31]

However, it is important to note the existence of a revisionist view which does envisage the possibility of socialism being achieved through a series of piecemeal reforms. Those who adhere to this latter view are usually described as *democratic socialists*. They are to be found in considerable numbers among the members of Labour parties of countries such as England, Germany and Australia. The basic belief is in the possibility of establishing a socialist state through evolutionary rather than revolutionary means. A socialist party is voted into power in Parliament and, through legislative changes, it transfers more and more decisions from the private to the public sector. Nationalisation of key industrial sectors is seen to be particularly important.

There has been considerable discussion among economists about the workability of a centrally planned economy in which decisions about resource allocation are increasingly located in the public sector, and the discussion has much relevance for the democratic socialist position. However, as Lange has shown, a centrally planned economy is quite capable of attaining all the conditions for optimal resource allocation, so long as the central planning board restricts itself to the setting of commodity and factor prices and certain other functions (such as determining the overall rate of investment and arranging the provision of goods to be consumed collectively).[32] Indeed, ironically enough, it seems that the democratic socialist organisation seems to provide a better vehicle for achieving the perfectly competitive pattern of resource allocation than the capitalist organisation, with all its attendant problems of monopoly, externalities and so on.

The difficulties with the democratic socialist approach are not so much technical as political. Movements towards democratic socialism typically follow one of two courses. Either the democratic socialists increasingly compromise with the property-owning classes who otherwise stand in the way of change, in which case the movement becomes weakened, less idealistic and less forceful. This has been the case in countries like Britain, West Germany and Australia. Labour parties in such countries, have typically been more 'moderate' in power than in opposition. As Miliband puts it: 'social democratic leaders, in their moment of victory, and even more so after, have generally been most concerned to reassure the dominant classes and the business elites as to their intentions, to stress that they conceived their task

[31] P. Sweezy, *The Theory of Capitalist Development,* London, Dobson, 1949, p. 249.
[32] See O. Lange and F. M. Taylor, *On The Economic Theory of Socialism*, Minneapolis, University of Minnesota Press, 1938. A useful summary of Lange's analysis is to be found in H. Kohler, *Welfare and Planning*, New York, John Wiley, 1966, Chapter 6.

in "national"; and not in "class" terms . . . (and) to insist that their assumption of office held no threat to business'.[33] The other course is for strong and sustained movements towards democratic socialist organisation to be sabotaged. Because any such movement is in opposition to business interests, it can expect resistance not only from the national bourgeoisie but also from international capitalist interests. The events in Chile between 1971 and 1973 provide the classic example, with the Allende government being subjected to various United States sanctions and C.I.A.-financed sabotage, leading eventually to its overthrow in a right-wing coup. Overall, it is becoming increasingly clear that the achievement of socialist goals is not possible through the so-called democratic machinery of the capitalist state. Rather, 'Wealth, both personal and corporate is perhaps the most important source of political power: and, in a vicious cycle, political power is used to preserve existing accumulations of wealth'.[34]

The Social Superstructure of Capitalism

The final major dimension of radical analysis is the appraisal of social relationships associated with economic systems. Orthodox economists usually avoid this like the plague, using various arguments ranging from 'that is the province of sociologists and/or moral philosophers rather than economists', to 'social systems are no more determined by economic systems than vice versa'. But radicals argue that such investigation is as appropriate for an economist as for any other social scientist. (Indeed the internal compartmentalisation of social science is seen to be counter-productive). Further, radicals generally take the position that most features of social institutions are ultimately traceable to the economic organisation of the society.

This last position is particularly central to Marxian analysis. The economy constitutes the base or substructure: the social institutions constitute the superstructure. The causal relationship between base and superstructure is complex but, generally speaking the direction of causation runs from base to superstructure. In a famous passage Marx said: 'The economic structure of society (is) the real foundation on which rise legal and political superstructures and to which correspond definite forms of social consciousness. . . . It is not the consciousness of men that determines their existence but on the contrary, their social existence which determines their consciousness.'[35]

[33] R. Miliband, *The State in Capitalist Society,* London, Quartet Books, 1973, p. 90.

[34] F. Ackerman *et al.* The Extent of Income Inequality in the United States, in R. C. Edwards, M. Reich and T. E. Weisskopf (Eds), *The Capitalist System,* Englwood Cliffs, New Jersey Prentice-Hall, 1972, p. 218.

[35] K. Marx, *The Critique of Political Economy*, reprinted in part in H. Selsam and H. Martels (Eds), *Reader in Marxist Philosophy*, New York, International Publishers, 1963, p. 186.

The reverse line of causation—from superstructure to base—does exist, but in a generally much less powerful form. As Hunt puts it, 'to argue that Marx believed that the economic base determined, completely and rigidly, every aspect of the superstructure is grossly inaccurate (although it is often done). He did assert, however, that the mode of production was the most important single aspect in determining not only the present social super-structure but also the direction of social change.'[36]

What follows is a brief consideration of some aspects of the superstructure associated with capitalist systems.

(a)   The character of *interpersonal relations*. The heart of the moral critique of capitalism has long been its impact on the character of social relationships between individuals. The usual argument is that capitalism brings out the least admirable aspects of human nature, such as avarice and aggression. Since the economic organisation is based on competition rather than co-operation one would expect this to spill over into social relationships too. Of course, some people consider competitiveness the most admirable aspects of human character, and these people normally favour capitalism for that reason. But for those who place a higher value on co-operative aspects capitalism typically appeals less than a socialist order. And this view is not confined to the freaks! Bertrand Russell wrote many years ago that 'the bad effect of the present economic system on character, and the immensely better effect to be expected from communal ownership, are among the strongest reasons for advocating the change (to socialism)'.[37] Even Lord Keynes admitted that capitalism 'is in many ways extremely objectionable'.[38]

(b)   The problem of *alienation*. That capitalist society alienates people from themselves, from each other and from their work has long been a theme of radical criticism (though it should be noted that Marxists are divided on the importance of this alienation issue). The term alienation is used broadly to describe the situation where man is estranged or cut off from that which is properly his. More specifically, the alienation of *labour* can be seen as arising from two sources, a high degree of division of labour, and the treatment of labour as a commodity. Division of labour, carried to extremes, makes work more repetitious and tedious. Even Adam Smith, the great advocate of speciali-sation as a means of increasing material well-being, recognised that 'the man whose whole life is spent in performing a few simple operations . . . generally becomes

---

[36]   E. K. Hunt, *Property and Prophets*, New York, Harper & Row, 1972, p. 75.
[37]   B. Russell, *Roads to Freedom: Socialism, Anarchism and Syndication*, Third Edition, London, Allen and Unwin, 1966, p. 133.
[38]   J. M. Keynes, *Essays in Persuasion*, London, Macmillan, 1931, p. 321.

as stupid and ignorant as it is possible for a human creature to become'.[39] Thus, alienation is in part a necessary corollary of industrial society be it capitalist or socialist. However, there is a second dimension which applies more particularly to capitalist society: the point here is that alienation is intensified by the system whereby labour is treated as a commodity, to be bought and sold in the market according to its potential contribution to capitalist profits. In Marx's words, 'What, then, constitutes the alienation of labour? First, the fact that labour is external to the worker, that is, it does not belong to his essential being; that in his work, therefore, he does not affirm himself but denies himself, does not feel content but unhappy, does not freely develop his physical and mental energy but mortifies his body and ruins his mind. The worker therefore only feels himself outside his work, and in his work feels outside himself.'[40]

The psychoanalyst Erich Fromm adds further dimensions of alienation. Consumption is one: 'the aim of buying and consuming has become a compulsive, irrational aim, because it is an end in itself, with little relation to the use of or pleasure in the things bought and consumed'. Also, there is the lack of participation by the individual in the forces that determine social policy: 'the anonymity of the social forces is inherent in the structure of the capitalist mode of production'.[41] Thus the individual feels alienated, not only as worker, but also as consumer and citizen.

Concern is not limited to the Marxists. The conservative Swedish economist, Staffan Linder, argues that material progress under capitalism has not liberated people for cultural and leisure activities, as its proponents contend. Rather, 'leisure time' is increasingly taken up with machine-maintenance and machine-oriented leisure activities in which there is little personal fulfillment.[42] Similarly, as noted in Chapter 6, one of the main criticisms levelled by E. J. Mishan, the liberal British economist, against economic 'progress' is the increasingly humdrum nature of work, and the relatively small range of jobs that draw on peoples' full potential and can be performed with enthusiasm and dignity. And in a funny sort of way, neo-classical economic theory backs up the Marxian critique too. The conventional analysis of productive efficiency —the 'how?' dimension of resource allocation as examined in Chapter 3 of this book—illustrates the inhumanity in the treatment of labour. It is a resource to be bought and sold in the market place according to its price and

[39] A. Smith, *The Wealth of Nations* (ed. A. Skinner), London, Penguin Books, 1970, p. 80.
[40] K. Marx, *Economic and Philosophic Manuscripts of 1844*, reprinted in E. K. Hunt and J. G. Schwartz (Eds.), *A Critique of Economic Theory*, Harmondsworth, Penguin Books, 1972, p. 105-6.
[41] E. Fromm, *The Sane Society*, New York, Premier Books, 1965, p. 123 and p. 125.
[42] S. Linder, *The Harried Leisure Class*, New York, Columbia University Press, 1970.

productivity, relative to the price and productivity of other inputs, such as land and capital. Yet labour is essentially different from other resources in that it is a human resource.

However, the over-riding aspect of the radical attack on alienation is its association with capitalist organisation. Sure, some boring jobs must be done in any industrial society, but it is in the nature of capitalism that even those in relatively privileged positions are subject to problems of alienation. As radical economist Herb Gintis puts it, 'alienation is not an aberration . . . not the private disease of the dissident minorities. In fact even the most timid and conformist capitalist man and capitalist woman is alienated from his society. It is the basic underlying alienation of *all* workers and citizens which gives rise to the modern malaise of advanced capitalist society. . . . Alienation is a social rather than a psychological problem at its root . . . (also) it results from the structure of technology only in the most immediate and superficial sense, in that the form that technological development takes is itself strongly influenced by the structure of economic institutions and their day-to-day operations.'[43]

(c) *Racial and sexual discrimination.* Sexism and racism are obviously not unique to capitalism. However, radicals typically argue that, while capitalism is not itself the cause of sexism and racism, it serves to perpetuate and intensify such discrimination because of the valuable function it serves. For one thing, discrimination is profitable, so that in a profit-oriented society one would expect possibilities of discrimination to be fully exploited. Hunt, for example, notes that in 1969 the wages of American women averaged only about 60 per cent of men doing the same jobs and suggests that 'on the basis it would appear that approximately 23 per cent of all manufacturing profits are attributable to lower wages paid to women'.[44]

In addition discrimination is sometimes said to play a further role in the stabilisation of capitalism. Sexist and racist attitudes serve to cause divisiveness within the proletariat so that attention is diverted from the more fundamental conflict of interests between the bourgeoisie and the proletariat as a whole. Baran and Sweezy develop this line of thinking as follows, 'each status group has a deep-rooted psychological need to compensate for feelings of inferiority and envy towards those above by feelings of superiority and contempt for those below. It thus happens that a special pariah group at the bottom acts as a kind of lightening rod for the frustrations and hostilities of all the higher groups, the more so the nearer they are to the bottom. It may

[43] H. Gintis, Alienation and Power, *The Review of Radical Political Economics*, Vol. 4, No. 5, Fall 1975, p. 2.
[44] E. K. Hunt, *Property and Prophets*, New York, Harper & Row, 1972, p. 170.

even be said that the very existence of the pariah group is a kind of harmonizer and stabilizer of the social structure.'[45] Thus, while racism and sexism are not part of a conscious conspiracy of the capitalist class, they play a role in supporting the existing social order by causing internal division within the proletariat.

(d) *Education institutions*. The educational system is another common target for the radical attack. The usual argument is that in a capitalist society the education system is elitist and technocratic, serving the needs of capitalist society rather than the requirements of human development. The education system serves this end by systematically selecting out (normally from about age fifteen onwards) smaller and smaller groups for further education, thus producing the required hierarchial structure. More generally, educational institutions are said to socialise children into the values that will secure a stable society, with the emphasis on routine, assessment, discipline (sometimes of a quasi-military nature) and the fulfillment of alienating tasks. In practice, many of these problems characterise education in socialist countries too: some educationalists, most notably Ivan Illich, argue they are inherent in institutionalised education, and that the answer lies in de-schooling rather than a change in the mode of production. However, it is hard to envisage how de-schooling could occur on a large scale in a capitalist society, since it would have effects quite inconsistent with the economic substructure. Indeed, this provides a good illustration of the general conflict between liberal and radical analysis. Liberals typically argue for reform in relation to undesirable features of the social superstructure, and look secondly at the problems of implementation; radicals look first at the economic function served by particular aspects of the social superstructure and thereby gain a more fundamental understanding about the relationship between economic and social phenomena.

Conflicts in Economics

This chapter has given a very brief introduction to the main dimensions of a reformulated radical economics. This is the sort of approach for which growing numbers of young economists in the United States, Great Britain, Australia and elsewhere are arguing. It constitutes a quite different paradigm to that of orthodox neo-classical theory.

The economics profession is quite clearly divided in respect of attitudes towards radical economics. American economist Robert Solow has described radical economics as 'negligible'.[46] Mansfield recognises the existence of radical economics but plays down its importance because it is 'so new' and

[45] P. Baran and P. Sweezy, *Monopoly Capital*, Harmondsworth, Penguin Books, 1968, p. 259-260.
[46] R. Solow, The State of Economics, *The American Economic Review*, May 1971, p. 63.

notes (with apparent approval) that 'the vast majority of economists would disagree with their conclusions. Most economists do not believe that capitalism should be replaced. Nor do they agree with the radicals' view of how our society works, or with their indictment of conventional economics'[47] (surprise, surprise!). Other prominent economists such as Galbraith have argued that the radical economists have given economics a long-overdue shaking from which hopefully it will never recover.

Of course, the radical reformulation of economics is very far from complete. Radical economics has received nothing like the attention devoted to neo-classical economics. Radicals typically have spent much of their time criticising the conventional view and defending their alternative approach, while neo-classicists have simply got on with refining their theories. (Indeed, in such an asymmetric situation it is sometimes a wonder that radical economics had flourished at all!) In recent years the situation has begun to change. There is a rapidly growing volume of literature which illustrates the determined effort to develop the theoretical and empirical aspects of radical economics.[48] Many problems remain, particularly in relation to the question of how to study aspects of economic power, how to assess the significance of social democratic reforms and how to subject to systematic analysis the transition from capitalism to socialism. Also, there are important unresolved questions concerning the nature of socialist organisations which will eventually have to be faced. Most radical economists are highly critical of aspects of non-capitalist countries now in a state of transition, particularly the Soviet Union, and look towards a more decentralised and libertarian system. But this raises problems of its own; the role of bureaucracy and markets, the role of material versus moral incentives, and so on.

Incomplete as it is, radical economics is of crucial importance, given the glaring need for a reappraisal of the state of economics. Any subject becomes unhealthy when it is dominated by one viewpoint for too long. Such has been the case in economics, which has too often been presented to students as a body of established facts and theories, seemingly almost above criticism. That stage is now over. The radical challenge, by exposing the implicit ideologies of neo-classical economics, by pointing to its constricted methodology and its narrow scope, and by providing an alternative framework of analysis has already made a major contribution. It has helped to re-emphasise that economics is a body of debate, not just about matters of business and government policy, but also about visions of society.

[47] E. Mansfield, *Principles of Microeconomics*, New York, Norton, 1974, p. 377.
[48] The publication in the United States of *The Review of Radical Political Economics* is particularly important in this respect. The United Kingdom has *The Bulletin of the Conference of Socialist Economists* as an outlet for articles on Marxist economics. Australia's nearest equivalents are *Arena* and the small-circulation journal called *Intervention*.

Author Index

Ackerman, F., 134
Alonso, W., 77
Arrow, K. J., 60, 72

Baran, P., 11, 68, 79, 102, 103, 115, 120, 128,
    129, 130, 137, 138
Baumol, W., 79
Becker, G., 121, 133
Behr, E., 3
Bentham, J., 104
Bierman, H., 93, 94
Bilas, R. A., 114
Boulding, K., 10, 22, 24, 31, 32
Brownlee, O. H., 113
Buchanan, J. M., 60
Buttrick, J. A., 113

Caplow, T., 109
Clark, J. B., 48
Commons, J., 121
Cyert, R. M., 43

Darwin, C., 105, 106
Denison, E. F., 9, 96
Deusenbury, J. S., 10
Dobb, M., 25, 26, 52, 73, 120
Dorfman, R., 31
Downs, A., 60
Dugteren, T., van, 86

Edel, M., 112
Edgeworth, F., 12
Edwards, R. C., 109, 116, 134
Embury, B. L., 116
Engels, F., 124

Frank, A. G., 128
Friedman, M., 11

Friedmann, J., 86
Fromm, E., 136

Galbraith, J. K., 3, 4, 52, 53, 67, 69, 100, 107,
    113, 119, 121, 126, 139
Garlin, V., 3
Gintis, H., 3, 137
Gordon, D., 106, 115, 116
Greenhut, M. L., 76, 77, 82
Gruchy, A. G., 121
Gurley, J., 56, 57, 89

Hamilton, D., 105
Hancock, K., 32
Harberger, A. C., 107
Harcourt, G., 50
Heilbroner, R., 103, 119, 126
Henderson, W. L., 75
Hession, C., 113
Hibden, J. E., 28, 31
Hirschman, A. O., 86
Hobbes, T., 104
Hobson, J., 128
Hofstadter, R., 106
Hotelling, H., 77, 82
Hughes, B., 32
Hunt, E. K., 104, 105, 111, 114, 122, 131,
    132, 135, 136, 137

Illich, I., 138
Iman, R. S., 68, 69

Johnson, H. G., 110

Kaldor, N., 119
Kaysen C., 126
Keynes, J. M., 102, 114, 135
Kohler, H., 133
Kolko, G., 116

Kuznets, S., 9

Laing, N. F., 50
Lampman, R. J., 127
Lange, O., 133
Ledebur, L. C., 75
Leftwich, R. H., 115
Leibenstein, H., 24
Lenin, V. I., 128
Lewis, W. A., 101
Lifschultz, L. S., 120
Linder, S., 136
Lipsey, R. G., 47, 73, 74, 117, 120
Lipton, M., 73
Locke, J., 104
Lundberg, F., 127
Luttrell, W. F., 80
Luxemburg, R., 128

McGuire, J. W., 11
Machlup, F., 79
Magdoff, H., 120, 128
Mandel, E., 120, 128, 129
Mann, H. M., 108
Mansfield, E., 108, 139
March, J. G., 43
Marglin, S., 97
Marris, R., 79
Marx, K., 119, 120, 124, 125, 134, 135, 136
Matthew, 35
Meadows, D. L., 98
Means, G., 121
Mermelstein, D., 116
Miliband, R., 133, 134
Mishan, E. J., 4, 25, 59, 69, 70, 99, 101, 109, 110, 117, 121, 136
Mitchell, W., 121
Morris, J., 3
Mundell, R. A., 83
Murphy, R. E., 68, 69
Musgrave, B. A., 116
Myrdal, G., 85, 86, 121

Nath, S. K., 25, 61
Nedler, M., 127
Needham, D., 68, 92
Nell, E. J., 50
Newton, I., 105
Nourse, H. O., 77

O'Connor, J., 131

Papandreau, A. G., 6, 72, 126
Pareto, V., 21
Parkin, F., 62, 125
Parish, R. M., 101
Passell, P., 101, 102
Pearce, D. W., 60
Perlo, V., 127
Petit, T. A., 69
Phillips, J. D., 102
Podder, N., 116

Radford, R. A., 32
Reich, M., 109, 116, 134
Reissman, L., 85, 86
Richardson, H. W., 77, 79, 81, 88
Robinson, J., 49, 123
Roehl, R., 3
Rose, A. J., 87, 88
Ross, L., 101, 102
Rothenburg, J., 97, 111
Rotwein, E., 11
Russell, B., 135

Samuelson, P., 62, 63, 83
Schmidt, S., 93, 94
Schumpeter, J., 107
Schwartz, J. G., 122, 131, 136
Scitovsky, T., 33
Sen, A. K., 28
Sherman, H. J., 114
Smith, A., 71, 105, 135, 136
Solow, R., 138
Stilwell, F. J. B., 80, 88
Stretton, H., 89
Sturmey, S. G., 60
Sweezy, P., 11, 68, 79, 102, 103, 115, 118, 120, 128, 130, 131, 133, 137, 138

Taylor, F. M., 133
Thirlwall, A. P., 84
Thunen, T. von, 76
Toffler, A., 100
Tullock, G., 60

Veblen, T., 24, 121

Wallace, R., 32
Walsh, V. C., 16
Ward, B., 61, 122
Warne, C. E., 68
Weber, A., 76

Weber, M., 125
Weisskopf, T. E., 109, 116, 129, 134
Williamson, O. E., 44, 79
Wilson, P. R., 116
Winch, D., 96

Zakon, A., 69

Subject Index

advertising, 23, 65, 67-70, 103, 109-110, 130
alienation, 99, 135-137
altruism, 97
Arena, 138
Association for Evolutionary Economics, 121
atomism, 105
Australia, 34, 86, 102, 115, 130, 133

backwash effects, 86-87
balance of payments, 8
benevolence, 24
black-markets, 31-32
bourgeoisie, 119, 124-125
brain-drain effect, 129
budget line, 19-20
Bulletin of the Conference of Socialist
   Economists, 138

Cambodia, 130
capital measurement problems, 48-9
capitalism, 4, 5, 23, 31, 50-62, 68, 72-74, 89,
   96, 102-103, 110, 114-116, 118, 119-138
centre-periphery model, 86-87
Chile, 134
China, 50, 51, 86
Church, the, 132
class structure, 117-118, 120, 123-126
cobweb model, 114
collective choice, 58-62
compensation criteria, 25
Concorde, 99
conflict, 25, 123, 138-139
conflict (or contract) curve, 18, 32, 41, 43
congestion, 75, 81, 87, 111-112
conspicuous consumption, 24
consumer sovereignty, 63, 69
convergence thesis, 52
cost-benefit analysis, 95

death, 96
democratic socialism, 72, 133-4
demonstration effect, 129
Denmark, 86
dialectical process, 123
discounted cash flow, 92-94
distribution of income and wealth, 29-30,
   48-49, 59, 115-116, 127
duopoly, 82

economic growth, 4, 6, 8, 9, 57, 96, 98-103
economic surplus, 102-103, 130
Edgeworth box, 12-14, 17-18, 23, 25, 27, 28,
   30, 32, 33, 39-41, 45, 50
education, 70, 90, 109, 115, 138
'effective region' of consumption, 16-17
egoism, 104
environment, 1, 3, 45, 81, 88, 98-103
equity, 3, 6, 25, 28-30, 32-34, 47-50, 51-52,
   83-85, 88-89, 114, 115-117
expected utility, 23, 92
exploitation, 120, 124-125
external effects, 23-24, 44-45, 65, 70-71, 81
   95, 98-99, 110-112

factor-bias effect, 129
factor-price equalisation, 83-85
false-consciousness, 125
feudalism, 5, 122

gerrymander, 2, 60
Great Britain, 86, 102, 115, 133

health services, 34

ideology, 56, 104-106, 107, 113, 120, 123,
   131-132
impatience, 97

imperialism, 14, 120, 127-130
income/leisure choice, 55-56
increasing returns, 113
indifference curve, 14-18, 22-23, 26, 55, 58, 91
inertia, 105
inflation, 8
information problems, 6, 23, 43, 68, 80, 87, 92
Institutionalist economics, 121
intellectualism, 104
interpersonal relations, 76, 135
Intervention, 138
investment, 87, 93-94
isocost, 36-37, 45
isoquant, 37-41, 45-46

Japan, 86

laissez-faire, 71, 75
localisation economies, 87
location,
—and efficiency, 75, 76-83
—and equity, 75, 83-85

macroeconomics, 8, 101-103
malevolence, 24
managerial revolution, 125-126
marginal cost, 54, 63-65
marginal product, 39, 42, 45, 46, 48, 79
marginal rate of substitution, 20, 21
marginal rate of technical substitution, 39, 42
marginal revenue, 65-67
marginal utility, 15, 20, 28, 57, 64-65
Marxist economics, 120-122-138
media, the, 132
methodology, 10-11, 139
metropolitan primacy, 86
migration, 84
militarism, 103, 127, 130-131
minimum wage legislation, 115
mobility, 6, 80-81, 89, 106, 108-109
monopoly, 6, 65-67, 82, 106-108, 113, 128, 129

nationalisation, 72, 95, 113
neo-classical economics, 4-10, 104, 119-121, 136, 139
net present value, 92-94
New Zealand, 130
Newtonian physics, 105, 106

oligopoly, 65-67, 82, 107

Paretian criteria, 21-26, 27, 28, 43, 69

people's capitalism, 126
perfect competition, 63-65, 79, 81
perfect knowledge, 32, 43, 80, 109-110
political process, 60-62
pollution, 75, 81, 88, 99, 100, 111-112
popular sovereignty, 117-8
poverty, 1, 116
pressure group, 61
price discrimination, 27-28, 32, 46-47
price system, the

—and choice, 72-73
—and distributional efficiency, 12, 18-21, 30-33
—and inter-temporal allocation, 94-96
—and location, 75, 78-85
—and the pattern of production, 53-54, 63-67, 70, 71-72
—and productive efficiency, 35, 42-47
—and resource allocation, 5-6
—problems of, 106-116
product differentiation, 73-74
production possibility frontier, 6-8, 54, 56-58
production techniques, 35-41
profit maximisation, 44, 51, 63-64, 75-77, 79, 92, 94, 98
proletariat, 124-125
property rights, 111-112
public goods, 70-72, 112-113

racial discrimination, 115, 121, 137-138
radical economics, 3, 104, 118, 119-139
rate of discount, 92-94
rationing, 31-34
redistribution of income, 33, 99, 115-116
resource ownership, 29, 124
resource utilisation, 6-9
Review of Radical Political Economics, 120, 138
risk, 87, 92, 94, 95, 97, 124

second best, the theory of, 117
separate facilities, 99, 112
sexual discrimination, 115, 137-138
social balance, 53, 71, 100-101, 116
Social Darwinism, 106
social objectives, 1-4, 114-116
social rate of discount, 95-100
socialism, 5, 31, 50-52, 73, 123, 139
Soviet Union, 50, 51, 52, 139
Spain, 35
spread effects, 86-87

State, the, 71-72, 106, 117-118, 131-134
superstructure, 134-138
surplus value, 124

taxation, 55-56, 115-116
technological change, 45-46, 75, 107
technostructure, 126
transitivity, 60-61

underdevelopment, 128
unemployment, 9, 67, 75, 114-115
Union of Radical Political Economists, 120
United States of America, 34, 86, 101, 113,
    114, 116, 125-126
urban crisis, 85
urban growth, 81, 85-89
urban structure, 77-78

value-judgements, 1-3, 28, 53
Vietnam, 130

welfare state, 33
West Germany, 86, 133
workable competition, 108, 116

Yugoslavia, 52